Home

Bring Your Child with Dyslexia, ADHD, Dysgraphia, or Dyscalculia Back to Their Natural Environment

**Copyright 2023
by A Homemade Education Press.
All rights reserved.**

No part of this publication may be reproduced, stored in a retrieval system, or transmitted in any form or by any means, electronic, mechanical, photocopying, recording, scanning, or otherwise, without the prior written permission of the author.

Limit of Liability/Disclaimer of Warranty: While the publisher and author have used their best efforts in preparing this book, they make no representations or warranties with the respect to the accuracy of the contents of this book. The advice and strategies contained herein may not be suitable for your situation or your location. You should always first consult with a professional regarding the homeschool laws in your state of residency. Neither the publisher or the author shall be liable for any wrongdoing on behalf of a parent or guardian when deciding to homeschool their children.

Homeschooling Wildflowers: Bring Your Child with Dyslexia, ADHD, Dysgraphia, or Dyscalculia Back to Their Natural Environment by Shelby Dersa
Paperback ISBN: 979-8-9882547-06
Hardcover ISBN: 979-8-9882547-1-3
Printed in the United States of America.
A Homemade Education Press
2025 Griswold St. Port Huron, MI 48060.
ahomemadeeducation@gmail.com

Table of Contents

Part 1: Homeschooling Wildflowers...5

Part 2: You Are Your Child's Expert...18

Part 3: The Foundation...34

Part 4: Supporting Needs & Respecting Growth...44

Part 5: Sowing Seeds of Interest...65

Part 6: Nourishing Strengths & Sprouting Passions...84

Part 7: Dyslexia, Dysgraphia, & Dyscalculia...95

Part 8: ADHD...138

Part 9: The Wildflower's Day...170

Part 10: From Surviving to Thriving...182

References...195

Acknowledgments...199

About the Author...201

Facebook.com/ahomemadeeducation

Part 1

Homeschooling Wildflowers

Wildflowers are not like the others. They do well in those unrefined places where society least expects them to grow...let alone flourish.

To "flourish" means to grow exceptionally well, especially in the environment one is meant to be in. For a decade, I've been able to watch my children flourish while being homeschooled. I walked into this homeschool journey thinking that I had to replicate a classroom environment. Like many, I thought the school work, the daily schedule, and the expectations had to be the same, even though I was choosing to homeschool for the very reason that the conventional method was not only not working, but did not allow space for my children to bloom.

Today, I laugh at the thought of how much I didn't realize in the beginning. Over the years, I've managed to create something so much more than what a regular classroom has to offer for my children who have learning differences. Instead of my children having to follow a standardized plan that was designed for numerous children to use, I've been able to provide a plan specifically crafted for each of my children in mind. When something hasn't worked for one of them, the learning path could be changed without attempting to change them. Homeschooling has allowed me to consider their feelings, interests, and their differences, instead of simply ignoring those factors because they don't fit into a particular environment that was created with only one teaching and learning style in mind. Not every flower can grow well in the same place and each one has its own unique characteristics and needs. The same is true for children.

I have been teaching my children for the last decade, and each of them have taught me some lessons in return. They've shown me that no one is behind or ahead of one another. I've learned that a child's progress is deeply influenced by concentrating on where they are at any given moment, as opposed to focusing on where they "should be." Also, we have figured out together that the secret of a successful education is that it does not have to look the same for every child, despite what society might have come to believe.

When children attend a traditional school, many expectations exist that must be met in order to be considered a successful student. From the time young ones start kindergarten, sitting still, listening without interrupting, positively participating in activities, and completing tasks in a set amount of time become the beams which hold together the foundation of their education. As time goes on, children are given information in a variety of subjects that require them to be able to process it as quickly and easily, like their peers. Not only do they need to process this new information they are consuming for the first time, but kids also need to retain it and show that they fully comprehend the material by relaying it back to the teacher in the method of the teacher's choosing. The expectations described may sound typical and indifferent to many parents. However, for a child who has a learning difference, these simple requests can become quite complicated.

Approximately one out of every five American children currently have a learning or attention issue, according to the National Center for Learning Disabilities. That is equivalent to 20 percent of all children in this country (Horowitz, Rawe, & Whittaker, 2017). The most common learning differences are also the least likely to be addressed at school, or will not be met with the proper support.

The four most common learning and attention differences are as follows:

1. **Dyslexia**
2. **ADHD**
3. **Dysgraphia**
4. **Dyscalculia**

Because of these, children who possess them learn differently than their peers. Many people confuse the term "learning difference" with learning disability, or think that it is a more dignified name to use in place of it. However, it is not meant to replace the label of learning disabilities. "Learning disability" is the legal term used when a person is diagnosed. Learning differences simply address the areas that some children learn differently because of a particular disability or other issues.

Learning differences can relate to the areas of reading, writing, attention, and math. For example, a person can have a hard time comprehending what they have read or can significantly struggle with spelling and the use of correct grammar. Some might not see numbers the way others see them and have a tough time manipulating them. Others may take a long time to organize thoughts and have to break down assignments into small chunks before being able to actually get started. This relates to executive functioning skills. A student who has learning differences has a differently wired brain than the average learner. This does not mean that he/she is intellectually incompetent. It just means the student needs to be taught differently.

The school system uses a one-size-fits-all approach to learning. If a child doesn't fit into a box, he/she will most likely struggle. Schools are required to help these children in the least restrictive environment possible. This means that students should be included in a regular classroom as much as possible beside their peers. The issue is that the traditional classroom is not designed with learning differences in mind and accommodations may not be enough to result in a meaningful education. Although there are specific laws in place to make sure that schools provide evaluations, interventions, and accommodations, they often do not follow the law. The most crucial problem is that many schools across the country do not have the resources to help these children or simply don't understand how to, which will be addressed in the next chapter.

One proposition to consider: if a school *did* offer services to a child with learning differences, would it be enough? When my son attended public school, he struggled so badly to stay focused on his work that it was often never finished. He was constantly being scolded by his teachers for not being able to sit still, stay quiet, and pay attention. He was the disruptive child that caused teachers to call me on a weekly basis. This is the same child who had an Individualized Education Plan (IEP). I attended multiple meetings to discuss his IEP and asked what more could be done to help him. The only supports they were willing to offer him were small-group test taking and a reward system based on his behavior. If he behaved decently, he would receive a high number of points as a reward. If he behaved "poorly" or not to their standards, then he might have received a zero for the day. The most problematic part of this system was that teachers never showed him ways to actually cope at school and they were not willing to teach him differently based on his learning differences. Obviously, teachers have a whole class full of students to teach, so the quick solution is to teach them all the same way.

Children who cannot learn the same way are forced to try to conform to the teacher's methods. As a parent who knows how hard it is for a child with learning differences to attempt to live up to the school's standard expectations, I chose to homeschool all of my children so that their self-esteem wouldn't be lowered, their personalities wouldn't be criticized, and so that their education wouldn't be pointless.

In recent years, I have noticed a dramatic increase in the number of homeschoolers, specifically after the Covid-19 pandemic started. But even though the surge may have been the result of a health crisis, many decided to keep homeschooling long after. The Homeschool Defense Association released an article stating that the number of families homeschooling was steadily increasing, despite the reopening of schools. Data shows that the percentage of households homeschooling at least one child or more rose from three percent to eleven percent (Duvall, 2022). When talking to new homeschool parents, I often hear them say how they wish they would have started sooner, or that they had no idea how much their child could thrive in a homeschool environment compared to where they came from. Some report their children having gaps in their education that they did not know existed. Others have confided in me about how mentally happier their child is now without the stress of regular school, especially for those who have some type of learning difference. Parents are becoming increasingly aware of the problem with how achievement is measured in schools, and they are not impressed. They are questioning the school system more and more. Most of all, they are questioning themselves. Can we do better as parents? Can we provide a superior education to the one that is offered? What do we want the point of our children's education to be?

About a decade ago, I was faced with these exact same questions. Then, as I had more children who each had their own individual set of needs and strengths, I realized that the ultimate accomplishment for their education I was hoping for did not ever align with a traditional school's. Although it might sound unusual to some, receiving excellent grades is not at the top of the list. Mastering every typical school subject is not either. Graduating with an official piece of paper makes so many parents proud, and I will be proud when mine graduate high school, also. But what my children had to do every single day in order to reach that accomplishment is what's most important. I will be prouder knowing that my children spent their childhood productively and more fitting to their needs.

In the end, the goal is for them to feel like they have received the necessary tools for their learning differences, to have made connections with much of what they have learned in a way that is meaningful to them, and explored their curiosity and interests wherever and whenever possible. Most of all, I will look back on their lives knowing that I strived for my children to have been given the freedom and time to push their own limits and to build a foundation for their lives which consists of real-skills, true talents, and many strengths. By the time my children's homeschool days are over, they will have learned not only how to cope with their learning differences, but how to embrace them. Their education will not be an exact copy of everyone else's, but will represent who they are, and will be completely their own. I will not settle for a childhood where they can simply grow well enough to survive. I want them to flourish, so they can thrive...and you are capable of making that a reality too.

Parents can either choose to fight with the school system on behalf of their children, or they can create something that most don't even realize is a possibility...their own learning environment that is crafted with only their children in mind.

What You Need to Homeschool:

A desire to homeschool, a yearning to provide a different kind of environment, and the willingness to learn alongside your child.

What You Don't Need to Homeschool:

A degree, a classroom, or prior knowledge of all subjects.

1. What does/will your homeschool environment offer your child that a traditional classroom cannot?

2. What beliefs do you need to let go of that are stopping you from providing an environment that will ultimately help your child flourish?

3. What do you want your child to gain along their homeschool journey?

4. What is the end goal for your child when they finish their education?

Part 2

You are Your Child's Expert

"ADHD has nothing to do with it, he knows what he is purposely doing."
- One teacher said about my son in regards to his inability to concentrate in the classroom.

Finding out that your child has a learning disability doesn't usually happen overnight. It's like slowly putting together a puzzle while trying to figure out your child, until one day you uncover the missing piece and everything makes sense. Then, the anger hits you because it took so long to put that puzzle together when the pieces were right in front of everyone. Why didn't teachers see it sooner? Why didn't they listen to my concerns? Why didn't other professionals ever mention that it could be a possibility? Why doesn't anyone seem to know much about this? The ironic thing is that schools spend so much time comparing children's test scores to see where they fall on a chart, but many have no idea *why* they struggle with certain issues that keep popping up. The frightening part is that many also don't even know the red flags that they should be aware of in the first place.

After my son had been in kindergarten for a few months, his teacher thought something was different about him, but she said that she couldn't put her finger on it. He had always seemed a little quirky, a little wild, and a little eccentric. He was definitely not interested in academics and would not sit still for anyone. He would, however, sit still for activities that *he* was interested in, to the point where he would become obsessed, and I would have to pry him away to get him to do anything else. At the same time, he was smart, affectionate, independent, and had an advanced vocabulary. I will admit that I was young and had very little knowledge of learning disabilities. When I thought of disabilities, I had a different image in my mind of what that looked like, and I didn't envision my son in that picture. However, the differences he had still led me to ask questions. Because of the positive traits that he possessed, my concerns were always dismissed. I trusted the "experts" and reassured myself that he must be fine.

When a child is young, a parent may not even realize that his/her child has any differences yet, or may not be sure that what they are seeing right in front of them is typical or not. Just because they attend school, it doesn't mean that the school will realize it, either. When assessments show that children are considered behind consistently throughout the year, it does not ensure that their teacher will automatically recommend having certain evaluations completed. Many parents assume that teaching professionals will catch and take care of any issues that arise, but that is far from the truth in several circumstances. It is common for teachers to not know the signs of many learning disabilities/differences, despite what parents may think.

    I do not believe that all teachers are completely ignorant about the topic of learning differences, but I do believe that they are not all trained to be knowledgeable enough on the issue. This lack of knowledge leads teachers to not only be unable to effectively help their students, but also may cause some of them to blame their students. In fact, the National Center for Learning Disabilities reports that forty-eight percent of teachers believe their students' learning struggles are due to laziness (Horowitz, Rawe, & Whittaker, 2017). There is a tremendous lack of understanding about learning differences on the teacher's part in many instances. As a result, these particular children are at risk of going undiagnosed and are instead described as lazy, disruptive, unfocused, and having behavioral problems. Teachers might recommend that the students try harder, when in reality, they are trying harder than anyone else.

In my son's case, I grew to wonder if he was showing early warning signs of ADHD (attention deficit hyperactivity disorder) since he could not focus long, if at all on topics he didn't want anything to do with. I had mentioned my thoughts to his doctor, but they seemed unconcerned because of how calm he was in that moment that he was being seen and also because his grades in school were considered to be passing. When second grade came, my son did not start to mature compared to the other children in his class. He could control himself for most of the morning, but would always let loose around lunch time. He would keep getting out of his chair, tap his pencil, make other noises constantly, repeatedly ask to use the bathroom, and he would barely stay on task. His behaviors had gotten increasingly problematic, so instead of just asking his doctor for her opinion, I had to be more assertive and request an evaluation for ADHD. After the doctor completed her evaluation for my son, she was quick to diagnose him, even though she did not take me seriously about my concerns before.

The Wait-And-Fail Approach

Some parents have a false perception of their child's learning differences. Some think that there is no problem at all, while others believe they will simply outgrow them. These beliefs can lead parents to not seek the proper help in or outside of the classroom. From the many experiences I've had with professionals, it makes me seriously wonder if a large portion of parents came to that conclusion because different professionals either told them not to worry, or did not give them the proper information about the signs of learning differences. More importantly, the "wait-and-see" approach often suggested by professionals, friends, or family, could've been a factor.

Sometimes, professionals may not actually verbalize to parents that they should take this specific route, but the fact that no action is taken after a parent voices their concern could contribute to the parents thoughts towards the situation. Parents might then go on to not worry for a while until it becomes apparent that certain problems are not disappearing on their own. In the meantime, other parents who second guess the "wait-and-see" approach usually view it as the "wait-and-FAIL" approach. They may know that something is not right and demand an evaluation early on. Surprisingly, they may find themselves hitting a wall when they are not given the proper support. Some educators will either straight up refuse to go forth with certain tests, or they will agree to conduct their own evaluation, but give inaccurate or misleading findings in order to avoid words like "dyslexia." Oftentimes, adamant parents who are doing their jobs as good caregivers will easily see the red flags that are consistent with dyslexia, dyscalculia, dysgraphia, or ADHD, and will express their observations with educators. But what happens when they still do not listen?

    A mother from Oregon spoke with me about how she had to fight for over four years to be heard. Her questions were never answered by the school system, but instead, an outside source. She was quick to notice that her daughter was having a hard time in kindergarten and did not hesitate to seek help. When the school that she confided in finally agreed to evaluate, they failed to recognize specific diagnoses and labeled her as intellectually disabled. The assumption that she was less intellectually capable than her peers led to her daughter being placed into a special education classroom. Her mother says that not only was her daughter not thriving, but she also hated going to school every day. This concerned mother finally received an accurate diagnosis for her daughter from a developmental psychiatrist, which included the four most common learning differences discussed in this book. Currently, she is happy to report that homeschooling has given her daughter the necessary time to slow down and work at her own pace in certain subject areas without having to stunt her growth because of the school's lack of ability to customize her education. Most importantly, her daughter is happy (L. Hendricks-Weissbach, personal communication, January 29, 2023).

A Diagnosis Doesn't Equal Help

Another issue to bring to the table is the fact that if a child is finally diagnosed with a learning difference and that difference constitutes them to qualify for services based on the law, this does not always change the viewpoint of a child's teacher or special education director.

One week after my son started third grade, the phone calls from his teacher began. She mentioned his behavior in the classroom and lack of effort he was putting into his school work. I told her about his ADHD diagnosis because she apparently didn't read his file, but she still didn't seem empathetic. I tried my hardest to talk to my son about his behavior that school year. I set up reward charts and communicated with his teacher often, usually because she was calling to complain. At one point, she told me his learning difference was not an excuse. It was clear that she was placing blame directly onto him and also onto me.

    Halfway through the year, a general teacher aide was placed into this particular classroom as a tool to help manage the children when any of them needed extra attention. My son ended up taking all of this teacher aide's time, and the teacher ended up assigning him to specifically help my son all throughout the day. After hearing about this, I promptly set up a meeting with his teacher and the special education director who manages the Individual Education Plans for students in that district. My question to them was, "if my son needs a person to follow him around all day in school, don't you agree that we should consider assigning him an actual special education aid instead?" I mentioned how it is not normal for a third grader to need this kind of support, and that he needs real help. I didn't want just any regular teacher's aide redirecting him all day or sneering at him when he was not listening. I wanted someone who could teach him how to deal with being at school all day and give him the necessary tools he needed. Someone with more knowledge could have had better methods of working with him, and it shouldn't have been handled like a punishment, which is how my son felt it was. The other factor to consider was that this particular aide was not going to be available the following school year. So, then what would happen?

With all of the good points I was making, the special education director shut down my ideas. She stated that because his grades were good enough, he did not qualify for any additional services. The ironic thing was, every test he took had to be written by the teacher's aide because my son was too fidgety and distracted to even write his own answers, not to mention his work took so much longer to complete, regardless of a person helping him or not. The special education director did not have a single accommodation to add to my son's IEP. Her opinion on the issue was to wait and see if his grades totally failed, and then they would consider taking additional actions. To me, he was already failing because his education lacked meaning. If a child's true needs are not addressed in a school environment, what kind of an education is that?

Who is Accountable?

There have been numerous stories from individuals, both adults and older children, who have learning disabilities that have described what life was like when they attended school. After reading many of them, the one similarity I found is that they felt "stupid" when they were children and as they were growing up. These individuals struggled throughout the years while trying to please their teachers and their parents. Some of them ended up with happy endings to their stories because it was finally realized they had a learning disability before they became adults. This may not sound like happy news to some, but for many parents and children, this comes as a relief to finally have answers.

Some children who finally do have some kind of validation—that their issues in school are due to factors out of their control—might go on to receive the help they need and have what some consider to be a success story, i.e. if that child happens to live in the right school district with the necessary resources. The truth is, less than half of students with learning differences will never receive help (Horowitz, Rawe, & Whittaker, 2017). Some schools may not have the proper screenings or evaluations to be able to find out if a student has a learning disability. Others may diagnose them, but they might not have access to the greatest interventions or are not knowledgeable enough to know what accommodations to offer. Then there are the schools who will not do any of these things and prefer to sweep certain issues under the rug. Many parents have reported that their child's school does not use words like "dyslexia," because the school does not want to label them. Or the school doesn't recognize the word because it's a medical term and out of their realm. It starts to become very unclear what the school system is responsible for or not. As a parent, it can feel like you have to become an expert on all the issues your child is having, because the professionals are not giving sufficient answers or solutions.

In 1995, the IDEA (Individuals with Disabilities Act) was passed. The law requires schools to find and evaluate students that could possibly have a learning disability and take care of the cost as well. This law includes children who have a health impairment such as Attention Deficit Hyperactivity Disorder, as long as their learning issues are affecting their school life. It also includes a category called Specific Learning Disability. Dyslexia, Dysgraphia, and Dyscalculia fall under this category (A History of the Individuals with Disabilities Education Act, 2020). The federal education system has passed legislation requiring the states to set up a plan for how to address learning disabilities in the school districts throughout that state. It shifts the responsibility to state legislators and depends on them to figure out how to carry out the evaluation process, interventions, and implement accommodations as they see fit.

Any typical person who reads about these policies would assume that because these laws exist, children who have learning differences or disabilities will have a solid chance at receiving the help they need and deserve. However, many parents of these children will say otherwise. The most crucial question to ask our education system is, "Who is accountable?" The laws are in place to make sure schools follow certain procedures, but schools blame the government for lack of funding or guidance that they need in order to effectively carry out these procedures. Even though schools are desperately in need of money, ironically, more funding is awarded to schools who have better test scores. So, the schools who have more struggling students, the less funds they will receive.

Let's say a school *does* receive a substantial amount of funding. The school districts will decide where and how that money should be spent. I remember back when my second child's school announced they would be purchasing Chromebooks for every classroom in large quantities, so they could use them as an additional learning resource. This occurred not very long after I was told that my older child could not be tested for dyslexia, and they did not offer specialized interventions for dyslexia at the exact same school. It may not always be about how much money a school district has, but it's about how they choose to spend it as well.

If teachers in public schools suddenly started teaching all the children however they see fit while using unproven methods, non-approved curriculum, and without following the education system's guidelines, there would be an uproar by parents and the rest of society. So why are we allowing schools to be able to do that to our children with learning differences? If the federal education system leaves the states in charge of planning how their schools will address the needs of children who have learning differences, and the states are not making sure every school in that state has what they need in order to carry out the duties they have to these children, then the chain of command should be followed. Therefore, the federal government needs to make a change somewhere.

Many parents are terrified to homeschool, even if they know their children deserve better. When a learning difference is apparent, they may feel especially unqualified to become the sole educator of their child. Oftentimes, when these parents mention the idea of jumping into homeschooling, negative feedback is likely to occur from some sources, and that can have a huge impact on whether or not they take the leap. If you join any online support group for homeschoolers with learning differences, you will find parents from all over who have similar stories about what life has been like for their children who have attended school. They will also share how they were once afraid of taking the leap too, and becoming their child's expert. The truth that many discover is that they were their child's expert all along, they just had to believe it.

1. In what ways do you know your child best that could relate to the way that they learn?

   Books to read, websites to research, videos to watch, and podcasts to listen to that will broaden your knowledge of your child's specific learning differences:

Part 3

The Foundation

"If a child can't learn the way we teach, maybe we should teach the way they learn." - Ignacio Estrada

The classroom is like a garden and children are the seeds. The gardener plants them carefully into even rows beneath the flower bed. They are expected to sprout, grow, and bloom all around the same time frame. Then, there are the wild ones. The ones who don't grow exactly according to someone else's plan. They may not do well in the place where the rest of the flowers do. They need something else, something different…as different as themselves. To an expert gardener, these living things might not grow in what's thought to be the best or perfect soil around. They might need to slowly get through the rocky areas or rough patches before they can eventually flourish.

A typical classroom has one purpose…to make sure every child who enters it remains on the same track. Teachers will measure where each child is at the start of a new school year, and they will continue to measure as time goes on. The curriculum is set in stone and the lesson plans are guided by it. If a child "falls behind" on the chart, or is struggling too much, a change to the curriculum is never suggested, unless maybe they enter into a special education classroom, which is not expected for a child who only has the learning differences discussed in this book. If a learning difference is finally discovered, the help can be very limited in many schools and still is not completely centered around that specific child.

In a homeschool environment, the purpose can be shifted from attempting to copy a standardized education and fighting to keep up with the expectations that come along with that, to creating a wonderful education that is homemade for a single child. An education such as this one does not only need to focus on weaknesses and struggles, but a large emphasis can be placed on interests and strengths. Certain techniques and interventions can be woven into the child's education in creative and unexpected ways.

Like a wildflower, when a child is placed in their most natural environment, they will grow best there. If they can be given the nourishment that is unique to their needs, they will go further than ever expected. When I use the words "natural environment," I'm not inferring that children with learning differences should be left to learn on their own naturally. I am telling parents that there is a way that they can guide their children in their most natural environment, and it will look different for every child.

When homeschooling a child with learning differences, there are three important parts to incorporate into their education:

1. **Supporting needs & respecting growth**
2. **Sowing seeds of interest**
3. **Nourishing strengths & sprouting passions.**

Take a moment to close your eyes and imagine what it would look like for your child to learn in meaningful ways without certain restrictions making that task difficult. Think about how good it would feel to soak up the joy that comes along with knowing that your child understood a new math concept without the feeling of still being "behind" weighing heavily on your shoulders. Contemplate how you could ditch some topics that you know deep down are not very important for your child to learn and that they will not make a meaningful connection to. Envision how those topics could be taken in a new direction that relates to what they are interested in, or replaced entirely, if you feel comfortable doing so. Consider the possibility of shorter lessons for more mundane tasks, but ones that you think are important for your child to complete, such as working on writing paragraphs when they dread the act of picking up a pencil. Or stir up some ideas for how writing assignments can align more with their interests, even if that does not mean sticking to a curriculum guide. What if a larger portion of your child's day is centered around what your child loves to learn about or having the time to build on strengths? That could mean taking specific subjects and finding the little things that spark their interests and zoning in on those. It could also be an opportunity to use current talents or skills and to strengthen them. This is what homeschooling a wildflower child is all about.

What is the Purpose of an Education?

If you search up the word *education*, the first definition given is, "the process of receiving knowledge," and the second is, "an enlightening experience" (Oxford Languages and Google - English, 2020). In society's eyes, the meaning of an education has become all about a specific destination one reaches in their life. To many, the act of a child fully understanding the knowledge they receive and actually applying it to real life is often overshadowed by focusing on the retaining of facts in a short amount of time and remembering them long enough to earn a decent grade.

    Educators have created an imaginary time table that children must live up to. Parents may tell their children that they need to get a good education if they want a decent job someday. Teachers might instill the value of receiving good grades into their students so that they will think about going off to a great college when they graduate. Administers drill the importance of studying and doing well on tests, so the school as a whole will appear well-educated. If an education is supposed to be about the process of becoming knowledgeable and making meaningful connections to what is being taught, then why is a score on an exam at the end of their educational journey what is most important? This result is so important, that the focal point of an education is now on students' ability to pass tests and show that they're progressing when compared to other students. The point of an education is not largely valued by the journey in which a child goes through. No one usually cares if they understand the background on a topic as long as they remember the basic facts to get them through their assignments. School awards normally only recognize top scores and perfect attendance.

What happens if a child cannot keep up or cannot connect the dots to make sense of what they are learning? Is the teaching method then changed, or are children told to keep trying to adapt to these methods?

I once bought a hanging basket of flowers that came with a tag attached stating they needed full sunlight to survive. I have the sunniest front yard due to the lack of trees, so I thought they would thrive in the spot I chose to place them in. I watered them as much as the instructions told me to, but a few weeks later I noticed they were starting to die. Even though the flowers came with a standardized plan of how to tend to them so they would keep growing, their growth was stunted. Instead of listening to my instinct right away, I kept taking care of them the same way, but with more effort. I made sure I watered them at exactly the same time every day, I paid attention to how much water I was giving them, and I left them in the full sun. You can probably guess what happened to those flowers. I set the pot next to the trash cans near the back of my house so I would remember to throw them away on trash day. About three days later, I came outside to drag the cans to the curb, and there lied the hanging basket that was dry as a tumbleweed just a few days before, growing a new pink flower that was surrounded by fresh, green leaves.

The well-known quote, "If a flower doesn't bloom, you fix the environment in which it grows, not the flower," by Alexander Den Heijer really is a true statement, yet it is hardly listened to. If you have ever attended an IEP meeting, you are probably aware of how the person in charge of the meeting will try to come up with ways for how your child can adapt more easily to the only approaches *they* offer. Your child can't sit still? Well, then teachers will let them have a three-minute stretch break every hour between the seven hours they attend school. Your child can't read at the level of every other child in their class? They will have thirty minutes of some type of reading intervention per day, but what about reading and writing for every other subject? Your child struggles with written test taking? Don't worry, teachers will give them a longer amount of time to complete their tests, as opposed to an alternative way to check their understanding of a topic. Your child cannot remain calm during a lesson or listen to instructions the first two times? They might be given a "sad face" on a behavior chart that is visible for every other student to see, as an attempt to motivate good behavior.

The broken school system sometimes convinces us that our child is the one who is broken, and we must constantly try to change them so that they will fit into a classroom environment. For my own children though, I have imagined something different. I have created an environment where they can be themselves while I can actively tend to their needs, nourish their interests, and watch their strengths grow. Their education is not about getting to a specific destination while remaining on the same road as everyone else, but rather an adventure where they can veer off the preferred path and soak in all the sightseeing along the way. A purposeful education has become the main focus in our homeschooling method.

1. In what ways has your child been expected to conform to an environment that was not designed with their learning differences in mind?

2. What do you think the purpose of an education should be?

3. What are some creative examples of how your child can model their understanding of a lesson or topic besides a traditional test that requires them to simply memorize a list of facts?

Part 4

Supporting
Needs &
Respecting
Growth

Every child's growth looks different. No one is behind or ahead, but exactly where they are meant to be.

Learning differences must not be viewed as a disability that causes the need of inconvenient accommodations or support that others are burdened with providing, but should be perceived as a different way of teaching. This concept would be ideal for many children and adults who are often looked down upon for their differences. Unfortunately, we live in a world where learning differences are highly misunderstood. There will be numerous, misinformed people who will judge your child at some point in their lives. These judgements may not matter in some instances, but there could be times when it does affect them. The most important person in a child's life who has the ability to see them as the wonderful person that they are and what they are capable of is most likely their parent or guardian. That special person can help a child see their strengths and work on their weak areas in a healthy way. They can team up together to discover what exactly the child needs and practice self-advocating. A child's home should be the first place where they receive respect and support for their learning differences, not an outside source.

Parents are the most crucial advocates and teachers in their children's' lives. They must take the time to research, read, and research some more, whether they homeschool or not. Sometimes the load of information that comes from all different directions can become confusing and overwhelming. "Should I do this or that?" Often, this becomes a recurring thought inside a parent's head. I have gathered many of these thoughts and laid them out for you in a clear, concise way. Evaluating these ideas for yourself will help you figure out how to respect and support your child in the years to come.

Meet Your Child Where They Are

Oftentimes, when parents have pulled their child out of school to educate them at home due to learning differences, they become preoccupied with attempting to catch the child up to the standards of the school system. They might contradict themselves by saying that their child needs to work at their own pace, but then worrying about where they are, standards-wise. All parents worry no matter what, that's a given.

But letting those negative worries pour out onto their children is a mistake.

The homeschool year could start out with a parent's best intention for success. However, it's important to remember what success really is. If you're focused on the goal of having your child be able to read at grade level as quickly as possible, be able to do math at their grade level by the end of the school year, or be able to concentrate well enough to sit down and complete three hours of school work at a table without many interruptions, then you may need to take a step back. Of course, all of those may seem nice, but they could be detrimental to your child's education and livelihood.

The core of a flourishing education is to instill a love for learning. In order to do that, it has to be centered around positive self-growth. Remind your child that they are only working towards being the best version of themselves, not better or as good as anyone else. True growth cannot be rushed. It has to be nurtured and taken care of with patience. Steps cannot be skipped in order to get to a result faster. Learning to enjoy every little victory will serve you and your child better in the long run. It will open doors for your child by showing them that learning new things, ideas, and skills are not a punishment, but a world of endless wonder and opportunity.

Never Expect Less, Only Different

Low expectations are sometimes experienced by children who have learning differences in all kinds of settings, but mainly in school. Normally, the intent that adults have when expecting less is not due to them trying to be mean, but is the result of either misunderstanding what the child is capable of, or even thinking that a favor is being done for that child. A quote I like to think of as a reminder is, "No one rises to low expectations," by Les Brown (Juma, 2022).

Although the goal of not leaving children behind or letting them fall through the cracks is often intended by schools, it happens more often than the rest of society would think. *The Guardian* has an anonymous blog spot called, "The Secret Teacher," located on their website where teachers can share their personal experiences without anyone knowing who they are. I came across a post from an educator who speaks out about how their school's leaders dumb-down the curriculum for children with any kind of special needs, including the ones who are clearly capable of learning so much more. For example, this particular teacher witnessed children with dyslexia read a thick novel during lunchtime, but reading books are not a part of the curriculum plan because the leaders in charge state that children with special needs don't like to read, so why push them to do so if it's going to make them possibly struggle? The curriculum given to special education teachers only includes the bare minimum of school subjects. This teacher also points out how the school uses tactics to make data appear that students are progressing, when in reality, the baseline of where the students start at the beginning of the school year are so low, that the charts will more than likely show progression at the end of the year (The Secret Teacher, 2018).

When a child with a known learning difference is part of a regular classroom that uses a standard curriculum, teachers might use certain tricks, so that grades will be considered passing. Since these students might struggle with the way the lessons are taught, teachers do not want to fail them when it is not their fault. Because schools do not have the time to work at a child's own pace or have the ability to customize the curriculum to better fit the individualized child's needs, teachers will pass them along from grade to grade, sometimes faking scores so that they will not be held back a grade. Oftentimes, teachers will score these students based on effort instead of outcome. Although this could seem to be fairer to these struggling students who have learning differences, this also leads to not providing the help children need to actually learn anything and progress. As a result, a great disservice is being inflicted on these particular students.

There was one point in time when I had considered enrolling my child into a charter school for eighth grade. I knew that high school was fast approaching and that fact was starting to scare me. Like many homeschool parents, the doubts were setting in, and I was overthinking about whether or not she was better off in a regular school for her high school years. I spoke with a guidance counselor about my concerns regarding her learning differences. I pointed out how a foreign language was necessary to graduate and how it would be very hard for her to learn another language when she has auditory processing issues, dyslexia, and dysgraphia. The counselor tried to console me by letting me in on a little secret. If my daughter has a hard time, the teachers would be very understanding about learning differences, and she would not fail because of that. The counselor basically told me that in order to solve such a problem, they would push her through and give her a passing grade instead of simply taking her out of that class and letting her take something else, so it's not a waste of time. Many parents might settle for a solution such as the one the counselor offered, or feel more at ease, especially if it's the only option given. The thing was, it was not the only option for my daughter. She was very interested in learning American Sign Language at the time, which this school did not offer. I knew she could excel at it and that it would probably be a good fit for her. So, why was I questioning my ability to plan her high school career when I could clearly provide a more fulfilling education, learning differences or not?

    I have spoken with other parents of children who pulled their children from school to find out that their children had learning gaps that they were not even aware of. One particular parent said that their eighth grader didn't have a clue how to divide numbers. She was stunned that this issue was never brought to her attention and her child kept receiving a passing grade in math while being pushed to the next grade level without being offered the proper help or guidance.

Sometimes, parents are told by other adults that it may not be the wisest idea to get a child's hopes up for college. They suggest that they take the easier way out and attempt something more at, "their level." Some individuals make the mistake of thinking that if these particular children take a more creative or unconventional route in life, they will never be as successful as their peers—as if there is only one path that must be taken. It sounds unbelievable that a person would write a child off like that, but some parents have been confronted by these comments even when their children are still very young.

In the 2013 documentary *Embracing Dyslexia*, a principal told a first grader's parents that they should face the fact that their child will probably grow up to be a garbage man (Macias, 2013). Comments may not always be as bold as this type of statement, but they can also come in more subtle ways, such as from family or friends who think they are not being rude, but realistic. They might mention something like, "your child isn't really college material, and that's okay." There are two issues wrong with these statements. One is that so much of society believes people who have learning differences shouldn't or can't choose certain paths in life, and the other is that they think only one kind of success exists. The only factor that could get in the way of a child with learning differences is not giving them the chance to grow in the environment that is right for them before they become adults.

Many students might not reach their full potential as a result of techniques being used in classrooms today. Does this occur in every single school? There is no way to say for sure, but it *could* happen in any school or in any classroom, and you may not even realize it. The homeschool environment is a safe place for a child with learning differences. They can push their limits as much as possible without being afraid of humiliation. Parents have more time to slow down and work on areas that their children are struggling with, instead of simply moving on. They can also make changes to the curriculum by substituting certain tasks and projects and going about them in a different way, as opposed to dumbing it down.

Choosing a Curriculum Based on Needs

There are so many curricula to choose from these days and many look so pretty and fun when displayed online or in catalogs. You might see other homeschool parents raving about the ones they use, making them seem appealing. Sometimes though, you will purchase one of these exciting curricula to later find out that it is not the best fit. It might require too much time, and your child cannot handle sitting still, or it may require too much reading or writing. There will be times when you're slapped with the realization that something is too advanced for your child or just plain not right, even though it's considered to be at their grade level.

There was a history curriculum I purchased once that was well spoken of by other parents. My daughter, who has dyslexia, started ninth grade, and I thought I had everything picked out, perfectly. I planned on doing a lot of read-alouds for history to ease the stress of her spending great lengths of time slowly reading the material. I also thought it would be a great way to teach her history vocabulary words because I could stop and further explain what a word meant since vocabulary words were a struggle for her as well. On the first day of school, I opened up her textbook and started reading. As the paragraphs went on, I realized there were not just a few words I'd want to stop and go into detail about, but a significant amount that I would *have* to stop and explain. The vocabulary was so far beyond her level, that it seemed like the book should've been at a college level for American History. I was kind of bummed out that the curriculum was not going to be very beneficial to her because I heard others talk about how great it was.

So, the new curriculum search began. I stumbled upon one that sounded too perfect. It was told in more of a story format to make it more interesting, and the store website said it could be used for late elementary and middle school, but also could be adapted for high schoolers. The samples looked amazing and were more at her actual reading level, so she would be able to read the chapters herself. I wanted to double check with other parents to see if they liked it or not, and the responses I got were things like, "oh that's a little below high school level, I wouldn't use that." At first, I was feeling bad that the curriculum my daughter could handle was viewed as not good enough. Then one mom left a comment that changed my thoughts. She said, "If the curriculum still relays the same information in a way that works for your child, then that's all that matters." She was totally right! That school year, history went smoothly, and my daughter learned a ton of new information using the curriculum I purchased and complimentary documentaries I picked out. As a result, she was able to effectively understand the concepts that ninth graders were expected to know.

Interventions & Accommodations

Sometimes, parents think of accommodations or interventions as techniques that only need to be used in schools, but that's not true at all. In fact, choosing to homeschool is already an accommodation in itself because by doing so, you are modifying their learning environment. Distractions, lack of understanding from educators, and teasing and bullying from peers are all things being modified right from the start.

Interventions are programs or curricula that are meant to intervene in specific areas and teach a child in a way that they need to be taught, such as a specialized reading program for dyslexics, a socialization curriculum for ADHD learners, or a special math program aimed at children who struggle with math or have dyscalculia. Accommodations can involve using tools to help the child learn, such as using audiobooks or speech-to-text apps. They can also include changing the educational materials being used, for example, switching out a textbook for one with much shorter lessons. As you dive deeper into homeschooling, you will find that by picking out certain curricula, enriching their lesson plans with other resources, and substituting certain projects for different ones, are a few things that can also be tweaked. In addition, more time and patience can be offered as an accommodation. If your child is at grade level in math, but not writing, it's okay to take the level of writing down a notch. Every adjustment that is made is a modification to your child's education.

Retention: Do or Don't?

When a child is struggling in school due to their learning differences, sometimes professionals or teachers will suggest holding a child back in their current grade. Even though research has been shown to not have more pros than cons, it has also been proven by researchers that it does not work. When a child repeats a grade, it might start off well at the beginning of the year when teachers are going over the easier repeated material that was already covered the grade before that and will be two times already for a child being held back. But as time goes on and things get harder and tougher, the same problems they were having before will arise again. This is because the root issues are not being addressed and are being handled in the exact same way as in the past.

It also will diminish children's self-value in the long run and not to mention, they will be surrounded by other children more immature than them, possibly, while their old friends have moved up. According to the research, children are more likely to drop out of high school if they were retained in the past, unless it was done very early on, such as kindergarten or early elementary level. Dr. Annise Mabry, Ph.D. of Tiers Free Academy, thinks that holding a child back a grade is never a good choice. "Grade retention does no good," says Mabry, "because it fails to address the underlying issues," (Epstein, 2021).

Despite the evidence, homeschool parents, especially newer ones, might feel an urge to have their child repeat a grade so they can have a fresh start and the pressure of playing catch up won't be there anymore. The fact is that their struggles will still be there. The homeschool environment is a perfect place for these children because parents can make many changes with specific school subjects. There is nothing wrong with having a child work on a different grade level for certain subjects. Some parents will even let their children advance to the next level on material that they are over-achieving in. With plenty of accommodations, children can remain in the same grade they were meant to be in while still progressing at the speed they need to in order to be successful in their studies. Your child's education is not a race against anyone else's, or even with themselves. Take the pressure off of yourself and your child, and just let them learn.

Life Skills

From a very young age, children with learning differences are constantly learning new skills to use in their everyday life. Not every new skill will come easy, and children usually have at least one thing that they are never quite good at. Although every child might struggle to catch onto specific tasks because no one is perfect, children who have learning differences often have a harder time with certain things that many others don't. It may seem obvious that if a child has underlying learning issues then people around them would be understanding of their weak areas and show patience. However, the fact is that many areas these children struggle with are not realized by even their own parents sometimes.

A learning difference can be compared to just the tip of an iceberg. Down below the surface, many issues are related to just one single learning difference. My daughter who has dyslexia has always struggled with the awareness of time and knowing what day of the week it is. I made the mistake of blaming her for not paying attention enough. I later realized that the simple act of memorizing the days of the week in the correct order was yet another struggle of having dyslexia. Parents have the job to learn all about the number of skills that could be affected by their learning differences. If issues are recognized correctly, teaching certain skills to your child can be looked at differently and taught more effectively.

Learning Styles

Most children can learn in a variety of ways, depending on the subject or task, but there is almost always a most preferred learning style that every child has. If you choose the best one for your child as often as you can, you will most likely have a better outcome with their academics and can use these same teaching methods to apply to regular life activities as well. If you are not sure which type your child is, you can find out by experimenting with different methods, observing how well they do with each one, and also see how much information they retain.

There are three major types of learning styles:

- **Auditory**: The auditory learning style involves hearing and listening to a lesson being taught, instructions being given, a task being explained, or participating in a discussion. Listening to videos, documentaries, podcasts, audio books, and oral lectures are great for these learners. They tend to be good at tuning in on a person's tone of voice, speed, volume, inflection, and also their body language. Allowing children to record oral lessons for the purpose of studying or retaining information can be beneficial. Teaching through the use of videos that they have access to playback is also very helpful. On top of being able to learn better using these techniques, these children also tend to enjoy giving oral presentations or learn better from reading aloud instead of silently.

- **Visual**: This style involves seeing and watching. Charts, diagrams, outlines, maps, presentations, lessons written on the chalkboard, and colorful, eye-catching illustrations relating to the lesson being taught. These types of learners are usually good note-takers or benefit from taking their own notes if they are mature enough. If the child happens to have dyslexia or dysgraphia, they may have to use non-traditional methods to take notes or have an already written out copy given to them, but it can still be a successful tool.

- **Kinesthetic**: These learners love anything that involves hands-on learning. They enjoy actively exploring, moving around, and touching the learning materials. These children are known to become bored easily unless they are doing something and often might even appear fidgety or restless when having to sit still. Some great ways for these children to learn are through experiments, crafts, science labs, building, constructing, manipulatives, and through field trips (Low, 2008).

It's Scary, but Worth it

I get it. Taking on the responsibility to homeschool your child can make any parent second guess themselves, let alone providing an education for a child with learning differences.

Thinking about the needs your child requires can be overwhelming and will make you wonder if you're fit for the job. From my experience, you might go from feeling confident one day to having that confidence completely shattered in an instant...and not only because of your own negative thoughts, but because of the words from someone else. If you go through with this educational decision, you will need to brace yourself and be prepared to hear the voices of others question your decision and ability to homeschool your child. Judgment or "concerns" might come from the most unexpected people around you and can catch you off guard. Remember that choosing to homeschool your child also means choosing to not care what anyone else thinks. Not relatives, friends, or strangers. Your child is yours to raise, period.

1. How can you meet your child where they are right now?

2. What criteria must your child's curriculum meet to ensure that it will work well with their learning differences?

3. What do you think your child's most preferred learning style is?

   <u>Research learning activities that might fit well with their learning style that you might like to try:</u>

Part 5

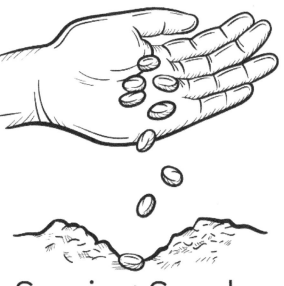

Sowing Seeds
of Interest

"I have found the best way to give advice to your children is to find out what they want, and advise them to do it." -Harry Truman

I have a memory from first grade that still hasn't faded away. Our whole class was sitting crisscross-applesauce style on the floor of the large library within the school, and I was in the very last row. We had been learning about insects for a few weeks, and I was pretty much over that topic. I was excited for library time because the librarian would always read a good book right before being able to stroll the aisles, looking for a book of our own to check out.

On this particular day, the librarian announced that the read-aloud she chose was a book about insects. Without a second thought I sighed and said something like, "oh man, not again." The problem was, the rest of the class was totally silent when I stated my feelings too loudly. The librarian then snapped back and asked, "Who just said that?" Without anyone having to say a word, I swear every single kid in that library looked back at me. I was then told to get up and go sit in the hall since I was being rude. The funny thing was, I was never purposely rude at school, especially to a person of authority. I did not want to get in trouble or be seen as the, "bad kid," yet I was treated that way for sharing my feelings of not being interested in bugs.

Do you remember the days when you sat in class, staring at the clock while waiting for school to let out? Or half falling asleep while watching the most boring video ever that your teacher put on? What about the time you were tolerating learning about a specific topic, but it seemed to go on and on and you had no interest in learning about it any further? Do you think you retained much information during those times? Do you think your love for learning was deepened? Probably not.

Interests and hobbies are more than just another way to spend a person's time. Incorporating them into a child's life is important for their well-being. They can help to raise self-esteem, confidence, and make life more meaningful as a whole. When these particular things are meshed together with a child's education, they become interrelated. Not only will the child become more knowledgeable of a specific interest of theirs, but they will also see how other parts of their education is related to it. Math skills are a must-have for woodworking or engineering. Computer skills are needed for robotics or graphic design. Economics should be taught if one wants to start a business, and so forth.

Making these connections will help a child to understand why they are learning what they are learning and will answer the old-age question, "Why do I have to know this?"

Interest-Based Learning

Interest-based learning is a method of education that includes using both personal and situational interests as much as an educator is able to. In the current traditional classroom setting, there is not much room for this type of learning. The most important emphasis is placed on teaching children what the school system agrees the children *need* to know, coming up with ways for them to memorize this information, and showing positive results when tested on these subjects. With current regulations, laws, policies, and the teacher-to-student ratio in American schools, interest-based learning would be near impossible to take advantage of, unless our schools are reformed. The good news is, parents don't have to wait for schools to change, but *we* can change the way we view our children's homeschooling education.

The interest-based learning approach can be used to get children excited about exploring new topics and in return, actually gain meaningful knowledge. Personal interests are topics or things that your child loves to do or learn about, such as dinosaurs, art, the *Titanic*, or computers. Situational interests are topics that pop up in everyday life or during school work that piques a child's interest. The educator has to be willing to adapt to these interests, and constantly tailor the child's education.

Personal Interests

We as parents love that our children find joy in certain things, but we often make the mistake of not taking full advantage of these endearments.

I had a conversation with a woman once about how her child was not ready for kindergarten because he had no interest in learning about numbers or letters. He only wanted to learn about what he was interested in. He had memorized many types of dinosaurs at only five years old and could pronounce the difficult names of them all too. I asked her if she had used dinosaurs within their learning activities. For some reason, she didn't think to do that. I suggested counting dinosaurs, matching colors with them, and even teaching the first sound of each dinosaur name. With almost anything being at our fingertips because of the internet, there are so many free or affordable resources that covers almost any topic as well. Educational printables with dinosaurs on them, videos using dinosaurs to teach the alphabet, or book suggestions come in vast amounts if you take the time to look for it.

My daughter always had a knack for arts and crafts. Most young children enjoy drawing pictures and finger painting, but her work was the one that often stood out. She had a vision for what she was creating and would hit the nail on the head with the end result. Being dyslexic and dysgraphic, expressing herself through writing was difficult while growing up. She possessed a great variety of knowledge and was genuinely interested in learning, but it was hard to show it in typical ways, sometimes. I soon found myself letting her make a work of art to show what she had learned when it came to history and science, in place of writing a paragraph about it. She created beautiful sculptures out of clay, detailed nature and Space journals, and drew diagrams using her digital art skills. Not only was she making meaningful connections to her studies that will probably stick with her for a long time, but she was able to branch out and explore her interest in the arts as well.

Adults often think of a child's intense interest as something positive, but concurrently thinking there's such a thing as spending too much time on one specific interest. It is thought that doing so will lead to them missing out on other opportunities or not becoming well-rounded. What adults sometimes fail to understand is that an interest is like a seed. If you encourage it to grow, it doesn't only go up, but spreads in different directions. Some might be surprised how far just one interest can grow or sprout completely new interests that they didn't know were related to the original source.

From a young age, my son was fascinated by how things worked. If an object had buttons, switches, or a cord attached to it, he just had to touch it. When he was four years old, he woke up early before anyone else and completely set-up my desktop computer that was still in the box. He also connected the interest cables. Everything was in working order by the time I had gotten out of bed. Through the years, he was obsessed with his computer. I tried so hard to get him outside or doing anything at all that didn't involve his beloved electronics. One day, his grandma gave him a robotic kit that had to be built. He spent all day long working on this thing, and woke up early the next day to finish. From then on, I tried to look for things that needed to be constructed. In addition to that, I started giving him any broken electronics I had or found some at thrift stores. He loved taking them apart to see what was inside. As he approached middle school, I purchased a soldering kit. He taught himself how to take apart electronics, rewire them to other components, and solder them together to make them work in different ways.

Personal interests are what set a person's soul on fire, young or old. Instead of teaching children to set aside these interests for small amounts of time because they have many other obligations to tend to, parents should make this time more of a priority. Children only know what they have heard before or seen, so with the help of an adult, they can be given more ideas or tools to take their interests many steps further.

Situational Interests

As you're reading a book to your child, teaching a school lesson, or taking a walk, something is bound to spark your child's interest. They will most likely ask more questions on the matter and carry on a conversation about it. This is the time you do not want to give short answers so you can get back to whatever it was you were talking or thinking about before. You can use these situations to do one of three things: offer to drop what you're doing and have a deeper conversation about the topic, decide to do some more research together, or save the idea and incorporate it into your child's school days, or any part of their day at a later time.

    My four-year-old and I were outside playing when he stumbled upon an ant hill. He observed the ants coming and going, looked at me, and without hesitation he exclaimed, "I want to learn about ants!" I knew what that meant. He wanted me to use this new discovery for a homeschooling theme. He was in preschool, so I would often switch out themes every couple of weeks. I used a sensory table, dramatic play set-ups, coloring sheets, simple worksheets or hands-on activities, crafts, and books from the library. Much of the time, I would use topics that I thought of myself, but if he became interested in a specific topic that stemmed from one, I would put the focus on that area the following week. For example, we were learning about the ocean. He decided he really wanted to explore the life of crabs more, so I picked up some books from the library, printed off some free or cheap printable activities, and found some videos about crabs for children. As time went on, he learned that if he was interested in anything at all, he could easily explore it further in a fun way. That's when he started coming up with ideas of his own from time to time, such as the ant topic. This has been yet another way to instill a love for learning.

What If a Child Doesn't Have Many Personal Interests?

I've heard parents say that their child is only interested in video games or so on. Oftentimes, children just have not discovered the thing that makes them tick yet. Or maybe if they potentially have, they didn't know how to go about learning more, or thought it wasn't possible for them to. Parents can help with this in a few ways. Whenever one of my children expresses an interest in anything, I'm quick to get online and search for activity ideas that are related to these interests. Sometimes, I can find easy ideas to start with, and other times, a child's interest may involve too much money to get started. If that is the case, I will either save that idea as a gift idea for Christmas or a birthday, or I will think of the resources around me.

If your child is interested in learning a new skill, but you have no idea how to teach them yourself, don't know much about it, or it costs too much money, think of possible people in your community who could serve as a mentor for your child. There are many individuals who are excited to hear that a child has taken an interest in something they also love, and are willing to help that child learn more. My neighbor, who is in his 70s, does woodworking in his garage. My son has talked in the past about wanting to make things with wood, so as an idea to get him out of his room and out doing something, I asked the neighbor if he'd be willing to teach him some things. My neighbor was ecstatic that I mentioned it. After a couple of weeks, they built a little wooden boat together. I'm not sure who enjoyed this activity more. Another time, my son spoke about mining coal, looking at rocks and minerals, which was sparked from playing Minecraft. So, I sent him with my brother, who likes to pan for gold in creeks and forests. My son came back with no sign of gold, but found a couple of rocks for his collection, and thought it was really neat to take little adventures like that. My brother said that it was hard to get him out of the woods that day.

If you're having a hard time with this issue, or need more ideas to work with, I've compiled a list of well-known or unique interests and hobbies for you and your child to explore. You can pick some for your child that they could possibly like, or talk to them about each one and see what they have to say.

Activity List:

- Fishing
- Kayaking
- Rock hounding
- Gold mining
- Metal detecting
- Magnet fishing
- Frog catching
- Maple tapping
- Bird watching
- Nature journaling
- Outdoor survival skills
- Archery
- Ax throwing
- Traveling

- Hunting
- Darts
- Gardening
- Conservation
- Animal tracking
- Geocaching
- Go-karting
- Four-wheeling
- Baseball
- Soccer
- Football
- Hockey
- Basketball
- Swimming
- Rollerblading/skating
- Roller derby
- Dirt biking
- BMX
- Skateboarding
- Ice skating
- Bowling
- Golf
- Disc golf
- Yoga
- Weight lifting
- Hula hooping
- Woodworking
- Carpentry

- Sewing
- Crocheting
- Knitting
- Embroidery
- Needle felting
- Weaving
- Jewelry
- Blacksmithing
- Welding
- Painting- acrylic, oil, and water
- Sketching
- Clay sculpture making
- Pottery wheel
- Ceramics
- Digital art
- Mixed media
- Furniture refurbishing
- Doll making
- Prop making
- Product design
- Stop-motion
- Animation
- Radio broadcasting
- Theater
- Anime
- Live-action role playing
- Magic tricks
- Card playing

- Chess
- Historical events
- Photography
- Scale models
- Costume making
- Special effects for movies/plays
- Makeup art
- Barista
- Cooking
- Baking
- Soap & candle making
- Illustration
- Genealogy
- Coin collecting
- Graphic design
- Museum curating
- Creative writing
- Non-fiction writing
- Journalism
- Book binding
- Blogging
- Create podcasts
- Make a graphic novel or comic strip
- Poetry writing
- Coding
- Robotics
- Computer programming, troubleshooting, or building

- Soldering
- Telescope building
- Star gazing
- Aerospace
- Ghost hunting
- Snap kits
- Home-built machines
- STEM kits
- 3D printing
- Architecture programs
- Entrepreneurship
- Marketing
- Content creating
- YouTuber
- Videography
- Disk Jockey
- Record collecting
- Stocks & investing

Connection Over Consumption

Previous generations of educators have come to believe that the consumption of information is more important than the connection to knowledge. They may not state that out loud, but the way children are treated shows it. A child's school day in a traditional setting is set up to fit as much information as possible in seven hours, alongside homework in many cases. They are also encouraged to participate in extracurricular activities when there is barely time to relax. Making good grades and staying afloat both at home and school becomes the forefront of a child's life.

In the documentary, *Class Dismissed,* children who were pulled out of school speak about the stress they faced before they started homeschooling. Parents stated how much their daughters loved learning when they were young and how curious they were to discover new information, until that feeling slowly diminished after attending school. Not only did these students begin to dread going to school, but they were faced with more work when they came home due to the immense amount of homework (Stuart & Woodard, 2016).

What are we gaining as a society by making sure children can memorize many things for assignments and tests, only to forget much of it soon after? By doing so, children are stripped of their interest in gaining an education. If children could slow down, dive deeper into desirable areas, and take the time to learn about what sparks their interest, imagine how many talents would be uncovered as opposed to making sure children learn as much as possible so they can become "smart." We would find that they are already geniuses in their own way.

1. What are your child's personal interests?

2. Think of a few examples for how his/her personal interests can be woven into his/her education.

3. How might you respond to situational interests in the future?

Part 6

Nourishing Strengths & Sprouting Passions

Children will discover their passions, if only they are given the adequate time to do so.

A child's strengths come in many different shapes and forms and are the pathway to a happy life. When a child has learning differences, they are even more susceptible to feeling down about themselves. If children grow up knowing what their strengths are and are self-aware of them, then they can use these qualities to their advantage. This particular kind of self-awareness will help them to understand what areas they are good at and how to use them in everyday life. For example, when a child becomes frustrated while trying to learn something new or is affected by their learning difference, they may come up with creative ways to learn by using their special strengths and skills. Another important reason for your child to know their strengths is because it will boost their confidence and self-esteem tremendously.

Over the years, my daughter's drawing skills have advanced before our eyes. She would become excited when explaining her illustrations to me and the story behind them.

Many of her sketches were attached to a plot idea because she had a passion to create vivid stories. I don't think she fully understood the depth of her talent though. Like many artists, she would compare herself to others. Her dysgraphia would also make it hard for her to get her stories down on paper in an organized format.

In order to encourage her to harness her creative strength, she needed to become aware of it first and realize what she was capable of. I kept my eye out for art contests and encouraged her to submit her work. She won the first three contests she submitted her work to, right in a row. After her confidence was boosted, she agreed to submit her sample work to a publishing company that was looking for a specific style of drawing. She received an email back that very same day, and she was hired for her first freelance artist gig at the age of 14. Her illustrations are currently being used in an educational workbook that is sold across the country and other parts of the world, displayed for many people to see. She has continued to focus on strengthening her skills in many different areas of art. At the age of sixteen, she was selected by an art studio for their teen artist mentorship program, where she was mentored by a professional artist and participated in her first gallery showing open to the public. If I would have made her spend less time doing art, and more time only caring about what I wanted her to learn, her skills would not be where they are today.

Become a Strength-Based Parent

Parents should focus a great deal on letting their children know what their strengths are by pointing them out. Doing so will help to outweigh their negative thoughts about any weaknesses. Parents should show appreciation of their child's strengths. However, appreciating them doesn't have to be done by just sitting back and admiring them from afar while wondering how those strengths will influence their future. Without your child even knowing it, you can help them to harness their strengths, talents, and skills in little ways. Doing so could make a wonderful difference in their life. I've gathered together seven categories of strengths.

The Strengths of Children:

1. **Social**: This has to do with the way children behave and interact with the people around them. Being able to follow

directions, respect others, including authority figures, being a good listener to their peers, being honest and truthful, and being a good friend are all social strengths. Parents can help harness these strengths by using plenty of positive reinforcement. Make comments to your children about what it is they're doing and why it's a positive part of their personality. Explain to them *why* these are good traits to have.

2. **Communication**: Children who are excellent communicators usually can talk effectively and listen intently to others. They may seem outgoing or not afraid to express themselves. They make good leaders and public speakers. They may have a large vocabulary and show expressiveness when they speak. Parents can encourage their children to use these skills whenever opportunities arise, such as when a leadership role opens up or auditions for a play are occurring. They can also be encouraged to get involved in helping their community in some way and using their voice to make a difference.

3. **Logic & Critical Thinking:** Children who have this strength could be great problem solvers. They may be able to solve math problems in their head, or quickly. Solving puzzles could be a skill that comes along with this strength, as well as being able to successfully disassemble and reassemble objects. They may be able to recognize patterns and enjoy investigating problems. Parents can plan activities that their child can do to put these strengths in use. Logic and mystery games, puzzles, scientific experiments, computer programming, model kits, taking objects apart, or activities that involve classifying or categorizing are all good ideas.

4. **Literacy:** This particular skill *could* mean that the child is an excellent reader and writer, but they could also be an imaginative storyteller, organize their thoughts for a story or research essay effortlessly, or be able to use an advanced vocabulary to express these ideas and stories. Creative writing prompts, short

story contests, writing a screenplay or a song, joining or starting a book club, poetry nights, filling in blank comic strips, or illustrating a story are just some ideas for children with this particular strength.

5. Learning & Study Skills: These include goal setting, being self-motivated, able to plan ahead, flexible thinking, learns from mistakes and fixes them, and is a self-starter. This strength can be put to good use by helping your child think of ideas for community and personal projects, business ideas, and so on. They might just need help obtaining the supplies needed for what they choose to do, but should be encouraged to do the thinking on their own and see what they can achieve.

6. Character: Children's natural characteristics come from within, and they were most likely developed when they were very young. Maybe they are empathetic, have a heart of gold, are very forgiving, have a good work ethic, are kind to others, creative, curious, always willing to help others, honest, or are very affectionate. Help your child become aware of their character strengths by pointing them out and discussing new ways to apply them to their life. Tapping into these strengths can help children be resilient. They can use these strengths for coping with life's stress. Talk with your child about times in the past when situations arose and they used those strengths to their advantage. Discuss how it helped. Come up with hypothetical scenarios for how they can be harnessed for the future. Another exercise you can do with your children is teaching them how to spot character strengths in others and talk about how those people are using them to live a happy life.

7. **Passions**: When an interest becomes so Intense that the child becomes skilled or very knowledgeable in the subject, this is when it becomes a passion or an acquired skill. Dancing, painting, hockey, yoga, cooking, gaming, or playing the guitar are all examples. The most tremendous way to harness these strengths is by giving

your children the resources, freedom, and time to pursue them. You should also show an interest in these things, even if you do not truly like it yourself.

Create A Passion Basket

Do you want to increase your child's motivation to accomplish their school work and give them something to really look forward to, all while being able to provide the time they need to fully immerse themselves in what excites them? I've created the idea of the "passion basket" where each of my children gets to have their very own. Every day when school work is finished, they pull out their baskets—filled with learning materials interesting to them or things my children are becoming passionate about. They are encouraged to use these baskets for the remainder of our school day.

For my son who is into technology and engineering, I include kits, graph paper, drawing supplies, duct tape and cardboard scraps, links to videos that I want him to check out that week, and a list of approved computer activities, such as coding websites or online classes. For my daughter who is into literature and art, her basket might include folklore novels, a book log and journal, links to art tutorials, a project she is currently working on, sketchbook, thesaurus, and creative writing prompts. Other things to include in passion baskets are books, documentary/video ideas, or fun worksheets and project ideas. These items may relate to topics that are from their school work and that will take my children to a deeper level. My belief is that children will discover their passions if only they are given the time to do so and are pointed in the right direction.

Influencing a Happier Future

It's no secret that children who have learning differences are going to struggle sometimes. These struggles can lead to negative thinking, and feeling like they are not good enough. This could result in giving up. Eventually, these children turn into adults and bigger problems may arise. By helping children identify their strengths and focusing their energy on activities that make them happy from a young age, they will be more likely to feel confident and worthy. The goal is for them to realize that their strengths always outweigh their struggles. Teach your children to never compare themselves to others, but only to who they were yesterday.

1. What strengths does your child already possess?

2. How can you encourage your child to hone his/her strengths?

<u>Think of materials you can gather to include in their very own passion basket:</u>

Part 7

Dyslexia, Dysgraphia, & Dyscalculia

"Some of us can struggle and thrive at the same time." -Anna Thorsen

Imagine being a young child, preparing for your first day of school. Everyone around you talks about how much fun you'll have, the things you'll learn, and the friends you will make. Your school days are filled with circle time, songs, snacks, crafts, play-doh, learning color names, and recess. For the most part, you're generally excited to learn about the world around you with peers by your side. But one day, your world is flipped upside down. The atmosphere of school changes. The expectations rise to a level that you cannot seem to keep up with. While everyone around you is learning to read and spell, you are struggling to learn the same concepts. Or maybe your spelling and reading skills are above average, but that doesn't seem to matter because you cannot catch on to basic math concepts. You sink down into your seat, feeling embarrassed and stupid, wishing you could disappear. Teachers become concerned that you're not trying hard enough or that you're simply not interested in school. They tell your parents that it will help if they double-down at home. Suddenly, home becomes a place where you feel ashamed too.

If your school does not have an early intervention program in place to spot dyslexia, dysgraphia, or dyscalculia, then the days of struggle seem to have no end and you go on to not understand why. The days turn into years, and you may find ways to avoid your learning struggles, such as pretending to be sick to get out of going to school. Eventually, a teacher might point out that your parent should look into outside testing or tutoring. Maybe your parents have finally put the pieces together themselves, and the right help is sought. For some children though, this never happens. They may become part of the thirty-five percent of dyslexics who dropout of high school, according to the National Library of Medicine. Another consequence of not receiving enough help as a child is the higher chance of becoming incarcerated later in life. *The Hill* posted an article discussing a study conducted in the year 2000 that took place in Texas. It found that forty-eight percent of prison inmates had dyslexia, which is an astounding statistic (Cassidy B. and Cassidy L., 2018).

Whether a child is diagnosed very young, during the middle years, or never, the educational goal is always the same for each of them…to catch up, to fit in, and to measure up to their peers in these specific subjects. This leads them to feel like their peers are smarter or better than they are. Almost never are they taught in school about what they are good at, or even better at in some instances. It is thought by many that children who have these specific learning differences are highly intelligent in the areas of entrepreneurship, engineering, architectural design, and the creative arts. If children are given the chance to explore these gifts further by including them in their everyday lives, they may become self-aware of their gifts. The shame of never feeling good enough could be replaced with feeling like they *are* good enough. They may struggle with some things, but knowing that they are talented or skilled in other ways might result in them feeling worthier. This could potentially make all the difference in their lives.

Teach the Way They Learn

When a child's needs are met in a way that has been designed for them, learning to work through their struggles may become a whole different experience. Combining the correct instruction with their interests and strengths can have extraordinary results.

My daughter has always been intrigued by a good story, despite difficulty learning to read during most of her childhood. During all of the elementary years, she could not read at grade level, even though she so badly wanted to hear the stories that lie between the pages of the brightly colored books displayed at the library. She was involved in a two-year dyslexia tutoring program that taught her the logistics of how to read in a way that she needed to be taught. Even though doing so helped immensely, reading a book would still be difficult for quite some time due to her reading fluency being so slow, making it difficult to comprehend what she had just read. As a result, I spent a great deal of time reading chapter books aloud to her, and she also spent a large amount of her days listening to audiobooks in her room while she was usually making art or doing other activities.

Eventually, she discovered graphic novels and how they were full of illustrations with short, easy sentences. This was the start of something great. On her own, she would slowly read a graphic novel. If she did not know a word, she would try to figure it out by looking at the pictures or ask me. She would also use Google to type in a word and then listen to the audio definition of it. Other times, she would skip it entirely and try to make sense of what she was reading on her own. As time went on, she would start to memorize how words were pronounced or would successfully decode the words using techniques she learned from tutoring. She became an advent reader.

I soon realized that there are an immense number of graphic novels based around many subjects, not just typical fictional stories. Some authors have taken a topic, such as, "The Sinking of the Titanic," for example, turned facts into a story, and was then formatted into the style of a graphic novel. You can probably guess what I did next…I started searching for books on the topics she was learning for school. Her education would consist of these types of books, videos, documentaries, audiobooks, and myself reading some material out loud. During the years when writing was so difficult for her, I told her to forget all the spelling and grammar mistakes for now. Writing class was just going to be writing. We would work on sequencing and how to organize a paragraph, even if it meant working on those things for a long time without moving on to more difficult writing tasks. Outside of this, we would focus heavily on vocabulary. Since she was not reading books on her own, at her grade level for so long, that made learning the meaning of new words difficult. This affected her writing, and life in general. The number of audiobooks and read-alouds she listened to played a very important role in expanding her vocabulary.

Eventually, knowing these words in her head made it easier to recognize them when reading simple graphic novels. After time went by, I didn't make her read to me anymore because all it did was hurt her self-esteem. She preferred to read on her own without help. I started to notice she was choosing more and more difficult books to read. Many were still graphic novels, but others were thick chapter books, National Geographic books, and classic novels. She would often tell me facts she learned or a plot to a story she just read. She was comprehending books that I didn't know would ever be possible for her to read. One day, I pulled out a book, pointed to a paragraph, and told her to read it for me. She read it clear as day, quickly sounding out the difficult words! Recently, I found her reading a novel that was three inches thick. I asked if it was any good and she answered, "not at all, but I only have a few pages left!"

Anna Thorsen, a dyslexia advocate, spoke wise words when she stated that struggling and thriving can happen concurrently, and it's such a beautiful thing to witness (Thorson, 2020). We often don't realize the simple things we take for granted, such as learning to read without great difficulty, or effortlessly jotting words down onto paper. If it was never a problem for ourselves, then we don't have a good reason to think about it... until we do. When our children have a difference that makes life difficult, we see their struggles day in and day out which can sometimes be hard to watch. We as parents want so badly to be able to fix their problems. But then the unexpected moments show up. The moments when we are first-handedly able to see our children burst through the rocky areas of their differences and show the world that they too can flourish. We finally become aware that our children don't necessarily have to be, "fixed."

The Real Effects of Dyslexia, Dysgraphia, & Dyscalculia

These learning differences affect reading, writing, and math skills and many children can have more than one diagnosis concurrently, or just one diagnosis while the symptoms just simply overlap with each other. When people hear the names of these particular learning differences, they usually think of someone who can't read, write, or is just bad at math. They may even assume that it simply means seeing letters backwards or all jumbled up. When a person has gone through being labeled with such a diagnosis or their child has, they will slowly learn that the learning differences affect so much more of a person's life than the rest of the world would ever realize. Parents who are just discovering a diagnosis may look back on their child's life and put the pieces together about how it had such an impact on them.

How Dyslexia & Dysgraphia can Affect Children:

- Not meeting developmental milestones on time that are related to language. For example, talking late, learning new words more slowly, having a hard time pronouncing words correctly, or mixing up sounds.
- Has trouble memorizing letter, color, and number names.
- Struggles to learn and repeat nursery rhymes or rhyming words.

- Is behind in learning how to read.
- Struggles to keep up in other subjects because of their difficulties with writing and reading.
- Has trouble answering questions on worksheets or finding the right words to use in sentences.
- Fails to remember the sequence of events, days of the weeks, or months of the year.
- Does not always see or hear the differences or similarities of the sounds of words.
- Struggles more than the average child when trying to sound out new or unfamiliar words.
- Trouble with spelling. Even when able to memorize how to spell a word, it is often forgotten a few days later.
- Is reluctant to read out loud.
- Often mispronounces words.
- Sometimes has a hard time understanding jokes.

- Summarizing or reciting a story is difficult.
- Memorizing facts, dates, or new vocabulary is more difficult for them.
- Some math problems may be difficult to learn, especially ones that involve many steps or having to memorize math facts, such as times tables.
- Trouble with spacing out words or letters when writing on paper.
- Erases mistakes often.
- Often uses incorrect spelling
- Has missing words or letters in their writing.
- Cramped grip on a pen or pencil.
- May have an unusual wrist or body position during a writing activity.
- Poor phonological awareness.
- Slow writing fluency.
- Struggles to copy visual information accurately.
- Inconsistent letter formation.

How Dyscalculia can Affect Children:

- Has a hard time connecting numbers to quantities.
- Struggles with counting, both forward and backward.
- Has trouble comparing two amounts together.
- Doesn't quickly recognize quantities of without counting.
- Difficulty memorizing math facts such as basic addition, subtraction, and multiplication.
- Has trouble with mental math problems.
- Unable to make sense of money amounts.
- Struggles with estimation.
- Has a hard time using an analog clock.
- Struggles to recognize patterns and sequences.
- Doesn't quickly know left from right.

- Lacks strong visual and spatial orientation.
- Has trouble remembering math vocabulary and symbols.
- Has trouble planning how to solve a math problem or finding other ways to solve a math problem.
- Has difficulty understanding units of measurement.
- Uses fingers to count instead of using other methods that they should already know.

Teaching Math

Dyscalculia is often a foreign term to many people because it is not as commonly talked about compared to dyslexia, yet research has shown that about fifty percent of children who have it also struggle with reading (Meldrum, 2022). Many professionals refer to dyscalculia as, "dyslexia with numbers." Mathematics is a challenging subject for many individuals. Some have a knack for it, and others do not. Sometimes, children have a problem with math concepts from the start. As they grow older, they may be deemed as a kid who is bad at math, or maybe they think they just strongly dislike math.

It is estimated that about five to seven percent of children in elementary schools have a specialized learning disability related to math (Jacobson, 2016). Dyscalculia affects the ability to learn and retain mathematical concepts, often making school difficult. It also can have an impact on other parts of someone's daily life, such as time management, scheduling appointments, playing strategy games, or memorizing the meaning of important symbols. If your child does not suffer from dyscalculia, but has dyslexia or dysgraphia, math can still be challenging in some ways. Children with these learning differences tend to have a harder time with story problems, memorizing math facts, or remembering the correct order of how to conduct certain math formulas, such as long division or more difficult tasks like algebra.

Since society views math as a hard subject, many assume that some children or even adults are just not good at math. This belief can oftentimes cause a delay in a diagnosis because a child's math struggles are not taken seriously enough or because the people around them are unfamiliar with the signs of dyscalculia. If evaluations that are meant to detect dyscalculia early are not utilized, children could unnecessarily have negative experiences at school or home and related to math.

Although it can be worrisome if your child is struggling with math more than expected, it's okay for them to pace themselves as opposed to rushing along to catch up. Many parents might believe that in order to get through math, their child must memorize times tables or every step to a problem no matter how long it takes them. Some brains have a much harder time with the memorization factor or sequencing steps into the correct order every time, but that doesn't mean they can't move on. If children understand the concepts, but struggle to memorize the information they need to know off hand in order to complete their math work, then cheat sheets could solve the problem. Cheat sheets might be thought of as something negative, after all, it has the word cheat right in the name. But is giving a person crutches when they struggle to walk, cheating? Is giving someone an audiobook when they cannot read, cheating? Is listing the parts that make up a paragraph when a child has dysgraphia, cheating? Giving a person what they need to complete a task until they are able to do it on their own is not cheating. If they cannot ever do it on their own, that's okay too. One thing I have come to realize from following this approach is that many times, something that was once a struggle solves itself on its own. For example, my daughter required a multiplication chart for a couple of years. After using it all the time while completing her work, she eventually memorized the times tables on her own as a result of referring back to the chart so often.

Whether children have a harder time with math or they are struggling at a deeper level, they may need a curriculum that allows them to visualize what they are learning in a more effective way. A curriculum that utilizes a multisensory approach could be much more effective than others. These techniques include touchable objects or things that can be drawn or seen.

My Favorite Curriculum for Math:

- Learn Math Fast
- Math-U-See
- Miquon Math
- Shiller Learning
- Ronit Bird's Math Books

Strategies to Help with Math:

- Talking or writing out a problem can help the student break it down and see the problem for what it really is.

- Another way to help the child see and understand the problem is to teach them how to draw it out. This can be especially helpful to visual learners.

- If a problem is more complex, such as having multiple steps before reaching the final answer, this can be overwhelming for the child. Showing them how to break apart the math problem into smaller math problems is key.

- Another strategy is to show the child how math problems pop up in everyday real-life scenarios. Also, using real-life objects, which we call manipulatives, that can be seen and touched are helpful for making those connections as well. Examples can include countable objects.

- The final strategy is to review previously learned concepts often. Even though your child may strongly dislike math and may beg you not to make them do a lot of it, they will highly benefit from daily review, along with new concepts being taught.

Teaching Reading & Spelling

If you have already done your research about how to teach your child how to read or spell, then you are probably no stranger to the Orton-Gillingham approach. This approach is the most highly preferred among researchers as an effective way to teach reading to both dyslexics and other struggling readers. The truth is that any child can actually learn by using this particular approach, and it has been said by professionals that it would significantly decrease the number of children who become behind in reading.

This particular approach uses a multisensory phonics technique that teaches a child the true meaning of letter and word sounds and the different phonics rules using visual, auditory, and kinesthetic (body-movement) teaching methods, instead of relying mostly on the memorization of words. It also focuses on starting out right where the child is, developmentally. If a child is in the third grade, but still struggles with recognizing basic word blends, then he/she will start there instead of worrying about which level of reading is to be expected. Lessons start simply and then very slowly become more complex. The parent/teacher also must provide direct instruction while giving continuous feedback and positive reinforcement.

Even though this is such a highly recommended strategy for teaching reading, it is not widely available in public schools today. This is due to ignorance and the lack of funds. It is also because most school systems do not intentionally set aside funds to increase teacher or special education teacher training, or to purchase the resources and programs that incorporate the Orton-Gillingham approach. If schools revamped the curriculum that they currently use to teach reading, every child could have a better chance at success. The success of students could also still be increased if schools only trained special education teachers to use this approach as well.

Many parents feel hopeless if their child's school does not provide good resources and learning methods that are needed for a better chance at real growth. They also might feel overwhelmed or worried that they cannot teach their child themselves. Luckily, there are programs that parents can purchase to use themselves that are based on the Orton-Gillingham method and give full instructions on how to use them. I've compiled a list of popular Orton-Gillingham homeschool reading and spelling programs that are affordable, easy to use, and are said to be effective.

My Favorite Reading & Spelling Curriculum:

- All About Reading and All About Spelling
- Barton Reading and Spelling System
- Explode the Code
- Blast off to Reading

Teaching Writing & Grammar

It may feel impossible to teach your child how to write a proper sentence, let alone a whole paragraph or essay. But it is possible, although the process may look a little different.

When teaching your child how to write, it's a good idea to focus solely on the actual writing part…not zoning in on spelling errors or correcting grammar mistakes. Save those things for their own time. This may sound silly because obviously in order to write well, spelling needs to be intact and the grammar needs to make the words make sense. Teachers would most likely expect the child to improve on these areas along with learning to write. Your child *will* improve in those areas as much as they are able to when working on those particular subjects, but this is not the time or place for it. Remember when I said previously, to expect different, not less? Taking out the spelling and grammar criticism and giving your child the freedom to simply study and learn about the process of writing a paper is one of the greatest gifts you can give them. It prevents them from dreading the already difficult act of writing as much. It will open doors to their imagination. They will limitlessly see what they are able to create, and you will be around to witness it.

    As a child grows older and their skills in grammar or spelling improve, it will show through in their writing. If those areas don't improve that much (for some people it doesn't), that's perfectly okay too. Accommodations including the use of technology can help individuals deal with these struggles and make life easier, which I will discuss later in this chapter.

Copy Work & Transcribing

When a child is struggling so severely that he/she can barely write down words onto a piece of paper, transcribing by a parent or other person can be helpful. Basically, as your children tell a story or explain a series of non-fictional events, you will write down everything that they say. When they're finished, read it back to them and then allow for them to make corrections or improvements about how something was said. If this is more work than you can handle doing constantly, there is assistive-technology that can do it for you. *Speech-to-text* is available for Google Docs and Google Slides and requires a microphone. Also, if using a mobile device, the program does not work, but you can still use your phone's built-in microphone option on the keypad when in the Google Docs application.

Before teaching children to write independently, a couple of techniques exist that will prepare them. You may be familiar with the term, "copy work," that is often spoken about by Charlotte Mason fans. Charlotte Mason was a British teacher during the 1800's who believed that children would become better writers if they practiced copying other great works first. For example, younger children would copy short sentences and usually older children would copy longer paragraphs from what were considered to be, "good books." Her belief was that children would learn directly from a source what makes a piece of writing well crafted, including grammar mechanics, organization, and how to breathe life into a single paragraph. For children with dyslexia or dysgraphia, this can be a great tool to use before diving right into learning how to write for themselves. It can also still be used simultaneously as the child improves on their skills overtime.

My Favorite Writing Curriculum:

- Brain Child's workbooks for kids with dyslexia
- Fix It Grammar
- Excellence in Writing
- Shiller Learning

Teaching History & Science

When people think about these learning differences and how they affect a child's education, it may not cross their minds how the differences can affect every school subject as well. Being capable of reading material, writing down answers, retaining historical and scientific facts, or memorizing the sequence of events and dates are all factors to consider. Having learning differences does not mean that every school subject has to be difficult. In fact, homeschooling has the power to customize these subjects in ways that many parents do not even realize, instead of the standardized way that we as a society have become accustomed to.

History and Science are often thought of as the memorization of boring facts, dates, and people that come from a dry textbook and the occasional documentary. Any child could have a hard time retaining such an enormous amount of information that doesn't seem to feel relevant to them, let alone a child who struggles with the skill of memorization. Reading independently can be even more difficult than reading other materials because of the constant new vocabulary words being thrown into history and science books, making comprehension impossible for some children. Showing what one has learned in the usual way such as with a paper and pencil can be an added challenge. What if I told you that having the ability to read one of those tedious textbooks does not define the success of your child's education? There is a better way to learn.

A couple years ago, my daughter was studying the Vikings for history. She was in eighth grade, which meant that knowing how to research a topic and then being able to present the findings would become a necessary skill to acquire. She searched endlessly for videos, documentaries, and books that she was capable of reading, related to this topic. I told her that instead of writing a long essay about the Vikings, she could present the information she learned in any way she chose. After a couple of weeks, she presented to me a clay sculpture of a Viking woman, one typed paragraph describing what she had learned, used spell check on herself, and then some other information was presented orally. I believe that her understanding of the topic had risen greatly by letting her study it in this way. It worked best for her in place of having a strict requirement that a traditional classroom setting may not have accommodated for her.

When searching for a history or science curriculum for your child with dyslexia or dysgraphia, locating one that offers audiobook or video lesson options can be helpful. Also remember that you can choose a curriculum, and then modify it as much as you want to. There have been times when I used a curriculum or history/science book simply for the sake of having a guide for which topics to teach in the appropriate order. From there, I would make up the assignments and find related resources. Being creative, and modifying whenever you see fit with the planning of homeschool subjects, is the key to a successful education for your child with learning differences.

Accommodations

If you are homeschooling your child, you're already offering him/her the largest accommodation of all. In a homeschool setting, the parent is able to test different kinds of tools and resources that can be thought of. The child also has an opportunity to experiment and see what he/she likes or what works best as well. The parent and child can then offer feedback to each other and gauge what the child needs more help with or what should change.

Although some accommodations can be put into place in a school setting, it's obvious that the options are more plentiful at home. Some may say that a child is not always going to be at home in every situation, so how will that help? Well, even though that is true, if the child wants to participate in activities or are in other real-life situations, he/she will know what works for him/her or parents can let whoever is in charge know what will work for their children. The same can be applied when the child grows older and wants to start working or attending college classes.

Since you know your child best, you probably already have some ideas on what accommodations they need, but maybe there are more that you have never tried or thought of. Choose the ones you want to implement, and if you find that they are not working or making any difference, throw them out and try something else.

Accommodations for Dyslexia & Dysgraphia:

- Teach typing to your child and let him/her use it for writing assignments. This way, he/she can focus on the actual assignment instead of their struggles with handwriting or spelling.

- Shorten writing assignments.

- Ignore spelling and grammar mistakes on assignments for other subjects.

- Let children give answers orally whenever you see fit. Instead of writing an essay or a book report, have them give an oral presentation of what they have learned. They can even get creative and set up a board with pictures, diagrams, or put together a PowerPoint presentation if they are old enough.

- Have them use wide-ruled paper for writing assignments. It's even okay to use the handwriting pads of paper that are meant for younger children if your child's handwriting needs that much help.

- Use pencil grips to improve handwriting.

- Instead of criticizing or mentioning how sloppy their writing is or how many spelling errors there might be, always acknowledge how hard they worked and give lots of positive reinforcement.

- Use a voice-to-dictation device or app on their computer/tablet when writing.

- Use a device that will read words aloud to the child. There are special pens that are able to do this and some even have a built-in dictionary to tell the child what a word means too. This could be a great tool for independent reading or to travel with.

- Let the child record a lecture you give, use video-based lessons that are offered online, or a homeschool curriculum that uses those types of lessons.

- Complete research for an assignment by using online videos or documentaries as a resource for their information.

- Listen to audiobooks that are at or above grade level. This will increase vocabulary skills, especially if your child is not fluent enough in reading books that are meant for their age yet.

- Have "read aloud time" even for older children or teens. Giving struggling readers a break and letting them sit back and listen to a good book with their parent will not only be an opportunity to bond with them, but will give them a chance to see reading as something enjoyable.

- Let your child skip having to memorize long, complicated sounding vocabulary words for science and history unless you think it's a really important word to know and remember.

- Place cheat sheets in their work area, such as math facts, directions for assignments that they have a hard time remembering, writing organizers, hard words they may forget and need to spell that week, and also having Google readily available if they need to look up the meaning of a word or how to pronounce it.

Accommodations for Dyscalculia:

- Provide cheat sheets with times tables or math formulas.
- Visuals for step-by-step instructions.
- Let children use calculators for certain parts of a math problem.

- Teach them how to use self-talk while solving a problem.
- Use manipulatives to teach math concepts, such as coins, blocks, or anything tangible you can think of.
- Show them how the math they are learning connects to real-life.
- Check work frequently and give feedback to make sure they are understanding or not forgetting steps along the way.
- Provide graph paper to help organize their math problems.
- Highlight key words on word problems
- Give extra time on math assignments or all the time they need.
- After giving directions, have your child repeat them back to you.
- Give more space to write out math solutions.
- Break down worksheets into sections or shorten up the number of problems given at one time.
- Use assistive-technology.

Life Skills

Children with these learning differences are capable of functioning intellectually well or even above their peers, but no matter how smart they are, there are plenty of skills that are affected by these learning differences in ways that most people would not even imagine. When dyslexia, dysgraphia, or dyscalculia are a part of a child's life, skills that go beyond academics can be affected, from social skills and communication, to the memorization and sequence of daily occurrences.

Even though your child might not be in a traditional school setting, there will be many places where they run into a situation where they need extra help, whether it's while they're at a young age, an independent teen, or growing into an adult. Maybe they are in extracurricular activities, a homeschool cooperative, dually enrolled in college classes, taking drivers training, or are applying for their very first job. Teaching children how to talk about their learning differences to others who may not know them well as early as you can will help them to feel more comfortable when they unexpectedly enter into situations where they realize they are struggling with something. No matter if someone has a learning difference or not, we have all been in a situation where we have felt vulnerable or embarrassed because we didn't know what we were doing, and were nervous to ask for help from a total stranger, especially if it's in front of a whole group of people. I imagine that for anyone with learning differences, especially children, they must be faced with even more of these types of situations, and this kind of thing can occur in the least expected settings.

When my dyslexic child went to a Summer day camp, her very first task when she arrived was to find her name printed on a sheet of paper mixed in with a long list of other names and then sign her name next to it. The problem was not that she didn't know how to read or spell her own name. She can do that just fine; she even knows how to sign it in Cursive. The problem was that she had to look for her name quickly while it was mixed between a bunch of others, and to top off the confusion, the names were listed with last names first, and first names second. She was skimming through the list looking for names starting with an "M" but couldn't find it. If someone without dyslexia had to do this task, they would most likely recognize quickly that the names were all last names first, and probably see their own last name without an issue. But not expecting this situation and being in front of strangers can make a dyslexic person frazzled. My poor daughter panicked and instead of asking for help, she signed her name next to a random one and walked away to avoid embarrassment....well that caught up to her fast and the teacher realized her mistake, then corrected it.

I left her there that day to go home and felt awful that I didn't think to prepare her well enough to find her own name on a sheet of paper, and I also realized that I did not prepare her enough to ask for help. Through the years I always read inspirational stories about people who were dyslexic to make her see that she can do anything and that it was nothing to be ashamed of. I talked to her a lot about her dyslexia, so she knew exactly what it was, but obviously, I did not do enough. The fact is, though, I cannot see every single situation she will ever be in. All I can do is prepare her the best I can, and a huge part of that is teaching her how to take care of herself when she is not with me.

As we all know, life doesn't come with an instruction manual, and learning differences can make life even more complex. I may not be able to design an instruction manual for you to use with your children, but I *can* compile a list of real-life skills that you can practice with them. The skills to start practicing with your children depend on their age and readiness, and ultimately, what skills you think your child still struggles with or what you think he/she should know by now. Some of these skills may not apply to your child at all, and might already come naturally to them. Since so many difficulties can overlap with these types of learning differences, I did not make a separate list of skills for each condition, but instead grouped them together.

Skill List:

- Telling the difference between left and right
- Using a map
- Finding a destination in a large or unfamiliar building
- Reading and comprehending instructions
- Physical coordination
- Estimating costs of items in their head
- Sticking to a budget

- Counting out exact change or giving change back
- Estimating time, such as how long a minute is
- Estimating how much of an ingredient goes into a food dish
- Comprehending and following directions
- Pronouncing words correctly
- Remembering a story or events in the right order
- Repeating a series of events in the right order
- Staying on topic during a conversation
- Expressing ideas in an organized way
- Listening and taking notes in a way that works for them
- Understanding body language and social cues
- Expressing feelings
- Knowing how to make friends and keeping relationships

- Memorizing his/her phone number and address
- Knowing the number for each month of the year
- Writing out the date in number form
- Keeping track of a calendar and dates of events
- Keeping track of time and scheduled appointments /activities
- Playing games that involve keeping score
- Memorizing math symbols
- Participating in activities that require reading or writing

Start by picking one item off the list, assess whether your child needs help in that area or not, either by asking your child about it, or thinking about past experiences related to the issue. If you are still not sure if it's an area of difficulty, have a practice run involving the activity. For example, play a game with your child that involves keeping score without telling him/her what you are watching for. If there is a struggle, ask your child about it. Maybe he/she can tell you exactly why they are having a hard time and it can open up a conversation.

Once you find something your child struggles with and you feel that they are old enough or ready to handle practicing the particular skill, think of ways this can be done. If your child is having a hard time finding his/her way around a large or unfamiliar place, then take your child out where he/she will be allowed to freely walk around and practice, or even make a conscious effort to let your child work on the skill naturally when you go anywhere. Going to the hospital to visit a relative? Let children do the talking at the front desk and have them lead the way as much as they are able to. Do they have a hard time figuring out change? Play a pretend game of "garage sale" and let them practice pretending you are a customer. There are so many creative ways to work on skills a little bit at a time. The important thing to remember is to keep it fun and light.

There will be times when children will be uncooperative or complain, especially if they have a really hard time with something or are embarrassed by it. Just remind them that they are in a safe place with you, and there's nothing to be embarrassed about. The reason you are having them work on certain skills is so that they will feel confident enough around others to handle the situation. It's also important to remember that they may not ever be proficient at certain skills. Even if that is the case, at least all of their incorporated practice will help them to be more familiar with different tasks, and they will know what areas they are weak in. You can then begin to think of accommodations your child can use throughout his/her life or how to ask for help from others.

Preparing for a Job or Career

Just the thought of sending your child off into the real world of employment can make many parents nervous, but those feelings hit harder when the child has a learning difference. Parents may wonder if other people will be kind and understanding towards their children, whether or not they can handle their new job, or if they'll be afraid to ask for help if they need it.

The first task as a parent is to not let your fear and anxiety fall onto your child. The second is to have an open conversation about certain job positions being more difficult than others, such as being a cashier when you have dyscalculia. The third task is to encourage your child to do whatever it is they really want to try, even if you don't see it being a good fit. Practice certain skills or reenact situations that he/she may possibly stumble across that could be difficult. Lastly, teach your child how to tell an employer about this/her learning differences and how to self-advocate if need be.

My daughter has dreams to be an author and illustrator. Even though her spelling and grammar (even transferring her thoughts from her head onto her paper in the correct order) would many times not scream that she should become a professional writer, I have heard her thoughts aloud and the way she tells a story is captivating. The images she designs to match her stories are those of an up and coming professional. Will I encourage her to pursue this career because that is what she wants? Absolutely! Will I offer her non-traditional ways to get her thoughts onto paper that maybe others wouldn't use? Yes! She has taught herself to use the voice command on her writing device and uses a spell checker as far as it will take her. She can go to others to help her fix more mistakes or to format her writing correctly. If she decides that she would rather avoid the struggle of writing and only wants to illustrate, then I would let her know that that is okay too, helping her down that path.

Let your child know that anything is possible, even if he/she has to take a non-conventional route to get there.

Wildflowers don't aspire to be the same as each other. Neither should people.

1. What curriculum would you like to further research?

2. What accommodations and interventions would you like to implement?

3. What life skills could your child benefit from practicing?

4. What else might you want or need to learn about, concerning dyslexia, dysgraphia, or dyscalculia?

Part 8

ADHD

"Children deserve to grow and learn in a place and alongside a force that is as wild and alive as they are." -Nicolette Sowder

A few months after I pulled my son from the public-school system and began homeschooling him, I mentioned to my son's doctor that since we started homeschooling, the symptoms of ADHD had declined significantly. I questioned whether his diagnosis was accurate at all. Then his doctor said something that hit the nail on the head, "Maybe he is managing his symptoms more effectively because of the environment he is now in."

When you think about it, the school environment is constantly trying to make children conform to their standards as a way to keep every student smoothly sailing throughout the years. For children with attention issues, there is no such thing as "smoothly sailing through" a traditional school's classroom. These particular children are often stripped of the characteristics that make them unique. Their education cannot be customized enough to work with the strengths they hold or the interests that motivate them to want to learn. Students are rewarded with approval from teachers and parents when they can hold themselves together long enough to complete a task, sit still, or not talk out of turn. However, during the moments when these children fall apart, they are told to do better, when all the while, they have been trying their hardest. What happens when the environment is changed to meet the needs and wants of who a child really is? Will they still struggle? No matter what, they will experience some struggles, but in a positive way that strengthens them, as opposed to beating them down.

Parents of children with ADHD often find that their children are able to concentrate very well on certain tasks when they "want" to. Maybe their unrecognizable attention span is longer during everyday enjoyable activities (ex: gaming). Perhaps it occurs spontaneously when the child discovers something new that he/she is interested in and starts a new project, such as building a model car. Oftentimes, parents might feel like their children have total control of what they choose to focus on or not, making them more likely to be less understanding of their needs. The term *hyperfocus*, is a common behavior among children diagnosed with ADHD. It's sort of like the opposite of not being able to concentrate at all. Hyperfocusing occurs when the child becomes very wrapped up in whatever they are doing because they enjoy it, or it is stimulating to them. Although it can be a positive aspect of having ADHD, people usually find it hard to stop the activity they are participating in. The good thing is that preferred tasks can be used as both interest builders and motivators in a child's education. They can also be managed in a healthy way.

Creating an environment where children can safely burst through their obstacles and grow to become the best version of themselves should and always be the greatest initiative. Forcing a child to adapt to an environment not made for them is like forcing a flower to grow in the wrong conditions.

A New Diagnosis Doesn't Create a New Environment

When my five-year-old wild child first started kindergarten, he hadn't been to a preschool or any type of daycare before, so I really didn't know what his attention span was like when being around complete strangers. I knew my son didn't like listening and paying attention to me, but it could've just been because *I was his mother*, I thought. Also, he was a little boy. How would one tell the difference between being a rambunctious five-year-old and a child who is struggling with concentration or not being able to sit still? Well, I would soon find out.

On the fifth day of school, my son's grandma was waiting outside the school doors, where his teacher exits with all her students. He did not take a bus to and from school, so someone always picked him up. As my mom stood patiently waiting for the teacher to release each child to their pick-up person, the line dwindled down to the last child, and my mom noticed that she did not see my son. She asked the teacher where he was, she looked around and then a panicked expression came across her face. "I, I don't know," is all she could say. They hurriedly ran back to the classroom and checked the halls. He was not there. After a couple of minutes, every teacher and the principal searched the school and an emergency phone call was placed. Just as the operator was receiving a description of my son, the teacher announced that they had found him. He was on a school bus!

Apparently earlier that day, the teacher explained to the kids that if they were taking the bus home, they needed to go up to the front of the class and take a little piece of paper shaped like a school bus. That way, the teacher would know which children to put into the bus line. My son, only being five years old on his fifth day of school and seeing other kids grabbing a cool looking piece of paper, took one too, not paying attention to what the teacher had said. Instead of the teacher not double checking which young children were supposed to take the bus or not, and the bus driver not doing so either, they depended on a brand-new kindergartener to know what they were supposed to do. They also did not take into consideration that some children might not be paying attention and that they do not know them well enough after five days to realize which children could have attention issues yet.

As the years went on, phone calls home were made and conferences became dreaded events. Up until second grade, teachers had not suggested that my son should be evaluated, even though he struggled in the classroom. I had him tested myself, and the diagnosis came back as ADHD. I thought at the time that having a diagnosis on paper would be welcomed with more understanding, patience, and interventions to help my son cope at school. My son's first grade teacher told me not to worry about second grade because she picked out the next teacher that she thought would be the best fit for him. That must have been a bad joke, because we were handed a teacher who had no empathy for him or understanding of what he was going through. She made it clear that she thought his behavior was due to a lack of discipline and that his diagnosis wasn't an excuse for him not to listen or complete his work.

That was the school year my son was also bullied by classmates. He began feeling anxious all of the time, and he was generally not feeling happy. That was also the year I knew it was time to bring him home…and it was the best decision we could've made for his childhood.

The Experience of ADHD

If you have tried to teach a child with attention issues a concept that they are not interested in, you most likely felt just as mind scattered as they did by the end of the lesson. They usually need constant reminders to focus, to pay attention, to stop rocking in their seat, and so on. I know how stressful it can be to teach children with ADHD, but how do *they* feel when attempting to start or complete school work? What do they experience in their everyday normal lives?

My son reported to me that he felt extremely bored at school and that there were too many things going on around him that would distract him. When we first started homeschooling, and I was getting a feel for what he needed to succeed, he would complain about the sound of the television that was on the other side of the house. He would frequently feel the urge to stand up and walk around. He always asked what exactly he needed to accomplish in order to be finished with school for the day. The simplest tasks took so long to finish, making the day drag on. There are many ways ADHD affects children, and it makes school one of the most difficult parts of their life.

How ADHD Affects Children:

- Problems with time management
- Seems like they are miles away or day dreams very often
- Difficulty staying focused on a single task
- Is easily distracted
- Gets bored with a project or task before it is completed

- Has trouble switching tasks or transitioning between activities
- Does not listen well to others, or at least does not appear to
- Has trouble staying organized
- Makes careless mistakes
- Seems to not pay attention to details
- Struggles to follow directions
- Is not good at planning ahead
- Leaves many projects unfinished
- Loses items or forgets things
- Moves around a lot and is very fidgety
- Relaxing, staying quiet, or sitting still are very difficult
- Talks a lot or excessively
- Gets upset or loses temper quickly
- Is impulsive and often acts or talks without thinking
- Intrudes on or interrupts other people's activities or conversations

- Speaks at inappropriate times
- Has a hard time keeping emotions under control or self-regulating

The Environmental Shift

Oftentimes, children who have ADHD and have either attended a traditional school or are homeschooled in a way that is meant to replicate a regular classroom, come to perceive learning as a negative act. If you start homeschooling your child from a very young age, it's much easier to prevent negative thinking about learning if done correctly. If you start the process of homeschooling later on as I did with my child, who has ADHD, it takes a lot of rewiring of the brain in order for him/her to see the joys of learning, and I am confident that a love for learning would've been deepened if we homeschooled sooner. The type of environment you want to create for your children is one where they can be themselves as much as possible. You'll have to take into consideration the setting, schedule or rhythm, how to implement school subjects, how you'll handle breaks, when and where to include interests and passions, learn what motivates your children, and the curriculum and learning materials you'll use. Whether your child has already attended a traditional school or you are choosing to homeschool from the beginning, the same factors should still be implemented in their learning environment, that you are now creating for them.

    The last day of public school for my son felt like a new beginning. The heavy weight of anxiety was lifted from his shoulders. I had wished he didn't have to experience that level of stress to begin with. Bringing him home meant more than just helping with his educational needs. You see, now he could comfortably be himself without feeling like a "weird kid" to his peers, or a "bad kid" to his teachers. Being home also meant working together with my son to find out how he could start and finish school work successfully. Boosting his confidence by being able to freely talk about the lessons was also a positive result of this new setting. Some might say that going from traditional schooling to homeschooling is a form of helicopter parenting or sheltering children from the real world. I believe that tending to children until they are strongly grown will give them the chance to both freely learn how to be themselves and to work on their needs. Homeschooling allows children to gain confidence and figure out who they are…before the rest of the world tries to convince them otherwise.

The Daily Rhythm

Many of you have probably already researched how to structure a child with ADHD's day. Practically every source will tell you to give your child plenty of breaks, such as 10-minute stretches and snack breaks in between school work. What if I told you a daily rhythm could be created that doesn't have to involve the word "break," besides maybe lunch time? It's possible to structure your child's day so that he/she can actually complete school work in a decent amount of time, participate in meaningful lessons, and have time to dive into his/her interests…all without mom losing her cool.

If your child does not wake up early enough on their own, come up with a fair time that will let them receive the sleep that they need, but also allow enough time to accomplish your goals for the day. Once your child arises, give him/her one hour completely to themselves before starting any kind of schooling or chores, but with one exception: they must get dressed and ready for the day. Getting ready can also include eating breakfast if they prefer. After the one hour is over, feed them breakfast if they have not yet eaten, or give them a small snack if they have. Doing so means that their belly will feel satisfied enough to be able to concentrate on work and prevents them from complaining if they are hungry twenty minutes after starting.

At this point, you may be thinking that the first task should be the least preferred one. After all, children are the most focused at this time, and you'd really like to get it over with. However, you will find that children will put out a much more positive attitude and willingness to start the day if the first activity involves minimal effort from them. As for myself, I read aloud during this time. My son is able to doodle and just listen. We all know how listening can be a struggle in itself for children with ADHD, so a listening activity prepares them for the activities that follow afterwards. If your child strongly dislikes drawing, give them a different but quiet activity to do with their hands. Towards the end of the read aloud, discuss with your child about what's happening in the story and what they think about it. This is not a time to quiz them, but just to have a nice conversation. Usually by this time, they will feel like engaging in a discussion, and it will get their minds working.

If you don't want to read to your child, other options are listening to audiobooks or watching a fun but educational video.

After morning time is successfully completed, THEN it's time to choose the least preferred subject. You'll move through each subject, saving the ones for last that your child is either really interested in, or any activities that involve him/her using their creativity. Doing so will give children time to take as long as they want to dive deep into the "fun stuff" or the things that spark their interests.

Short but Meaningful Lessons

Connection over consumption is the secret to always remember. It's normal for homeschool parents to sometimes feel like their child is not doing or learning enough. When other children are at school for six or seven hours out of the day and your core-subject lessons with your homeschooled children only take an hour and a half, you might begin to question yourself. Those doubtful thoughts might turn into implementing a heavier workload for your children, just so you can feel like you're doing a better job of educating them. The truth is, when too much is thrown at children in a day, only tiny fragments of what was taught are actually going to stick with them. If your children are actually given the time to place all of their attention and focus on less areas per day, the connection to what they are learning will be stronger. Children with ADHD can only successfully concentrate on so much at a time, anyways, so this method of teaching works well for them.

If you'd like to be able to move through each subject quickly and effortlessly without having to take a lot of breaks, keep most lessons short, yet meaningful. The younger the child is, the shorter the lesson should be. This will most likely not be possible if you choose the wrong curriculum. This is why I do not suggest choosing a "big box curriculum" (gives you a complete program for every subject). A curriculum such as this is too difficult to customize or shorten the lessons enough without leaving holes or gaps in learning. Choosing a curriculum for each subject that already has short lessons is the first step in the right direction. If the lessons are a little longer than you'd like them to be or have extra practice pages that are repetitive, then simply throw out those unneeded activities. You will find that plenty of educational materials contain a lot of extra "fluff." Remember that your home is not a classroom requiring students to complete busy work just to simply fill in time, while other children are still working.

Altering Lessons to Serve Interests

Many times, an opportunity for deeper learning can be missed because we as our child's teacher decide to firmly stick to an assignment. Take language arts for instance. A writing activity instructs children to write a persuasive paragraph about whether or not they think zoos should be allowed to house wild animals, or instead should let the animals be in their most natural environment. Maybe it is perceived as a boring subject. If so, do you think that children will put much thought into their paragraph, or provide sloppy/minimal work just to get through it? They might be so unengaged that they do not concentrate at all, and waste the day away. What if your child is particularly upset that circuses are allowed to keep wild animals? Or maybe your child is interested in making some kind of environmental change elsewhere? As long as you keep the purpose of the assignment the same, but change the content, the purpose will not only be fulfilled but probably increase your child's knowledge on a specific topic that he or she will actually remember down the road. Most likely, writing skills will be affected more positively, too.

Substituting Lessons for Hands-On Experiences

Oftentimes, people think of hands-on learning as science experiments or big, time-consuming projects. In reality, there are so many easy opportunities for learning through other resources. If you choose a history topic on your child's agenda and type it into an online search along with the key words, "hands-on," you will find many ways to make lessons come alive. Many are free ideas you can do with your own supplies. Printable resources can be very cost effective as well. When my children were learning about ancient Roman gladiators, I found a printable board game based around that topic. Three dollars for the purchase, four pages from the printer, and some cutting allowed me time off from having to quiz my kids on a bunch of facts and instead, had them learn new information for themselves while being entertained. Another example is when I was teaching my daughter the concept of area and perimeter in math. I supplied her with large square graph paper and told her to design a layout of a house. After that, we moved on to a 3D house using scissors and scotch tape to piece it together. The concept was learned much more easily and with more enthusiasm, which always makes a big difference.

Honing Their Unique Strengths

Medical News Today wrote these words while discussing ADHD: "The best way to make the most of ADHD superpowers is to manage the person's environment in order to allow them to flourish" (Sherrell, 2021). What abilities are they talking about exactly? Hyperfocusing, resiliency, conversational skills, and high energy levels are the strengths that children with ADHD have, but most of those strengths are considered problems in a traditional educational setting. A homeschool setting allows for a child to use his/her skills to the best of his/her abilities, while also learning within a safe setting how to manage any negative side effects of these special characteristics.

A couple of important attributes of people who accomplish their goals is having perseverance and resilience. Sticking it out and completing multiple tasks in order to get a project done is oftentimes the key that many individuals do not hold. Life gets in the way such as unexpected hurdles and setbacks, making it easy to put goals on the back burner for too long, or to feel beaten down and never get back to them at all. However, for people with ADHD who are passionate about something in their lives, that drive they have, stemming from their hyperfocused abilities and resiliency, is what can set them apart from others. Sure, this super power may be annoying to others at times when they are trying to pry these children away from a project, but it's also amazing to witness, and it's a skill that should be celebrated and taken advantage of.

    Children who have ADHD might be sneered at for talking in class or judged by their peers for talking too much. However, these particular outgoing conversational skills and ability to speak up easily and effortlessly is a strength that many others wish they had in certain situations. Making friends, building relationships, and having open communication with others is far easier to do when your speaking skills are up to par. Some might not click well with such a seemingly extroverted personality type, but the ones who do are the right friends for them anyways. The classroom is viewed as a place to learn how to be quiet when needed, to speak when expected to, and to follow directions without causing distractions to others. It is thought that classrooms prepare children for the college setting and the workforce. One thing is forgotten though...the fact that children mature as they grow, and realizing that you cannot openly talk while a teacher, peers, coworkers, or their supervisors are talking, is an acquired skill they will gain on their own, and maybe with a little awareness from others who care about them along the way.

Expecting a child with ADHD or any child for that matter to constantly sit and be quiet for so many hours per day is not only unfair to that child, but also hinders their expressiveness and communication skills when they should be honed and dealt with differently. After all, being able to converse with others easily and smoothly is a characteristic that most employers look for, and a trait that peers appreciate.

The phrase "bouncing off the walls" is often used to describe hyperactive children. The truth is that a regular classroom is simply not equipped to handle children who are more physically energetic than others, because it was not designed to do so. Giving children the time and space to be physically active along with hands-on learning activities that meet their sensory needs are crucial for a child with ADHD. Instead of attempting to squash their high energy level, let them use it. When they grow up, maybe they'll be able to handle a desk job, or maybe they won't. Either way, jobs or activities that involve sitting still are only some of the options that are out there and physically active roles exist.

Homeschool Curriculum & Learning Materials

There are some curriculum programs that keep ADHD in mind, or ones that are a better fit than others. No matter the curriculum chosen, if you want one that will most likely fit specific needs, there are certain things to look for. A curriculum that provides short lessons will be the most important factor, unless it's an area of high interest. Forty-five minutes to an hour long for each subject will most likely not be a good fit. My advice would be to aim for fifteen to twenty minutes in the subjects that your child is not the most excited about or that they struggle with.

The other factor that plays a role in a great curriculum is the opportunity for flexibility. Are there options for which activities or exercises to do so your child has more choices? Or is it easy to substitute certain aspects of it for something different (or for a hands-on activity)? Can your child use his/her interests as a guide toward particular activities, projects, research, or reports, or is everything chosen for them?

The last factor to consider is if it is possible to make accommodations while using the curriculum. For example, does the curriculum require that your child read a whole chapter book in a week or two, even though it might take your child much longer due to not being able to sit still for that long? Does it require your child to complete two whole pages of math problems every day, even though they can only handle one? Will they often need to read a large portion from their history or science book independently and answer questions, instead of being able to break it up more without taking too long to complete the entire book in a school year? The important thing to remember is to not set your child up for failure, just because you like the curriculum and think it would be good for your child to do specific types of work. I've compiled a list of different homeschool learning materials, ideas, and curriculum, more engaging than others.

Hands-On Learning Ideas and Materials:

- Interactive journals and lapbooks f
- Online games
- Games such as bingo or find-the-match
- Hands-on history projects
- Cook recipes based on a certain time period or culture
- Put together a timeline to hang up
- Math manipulatives
- Use Legos, pizza, or other real-life objects to teach fractions
- Create a house blueprint on graph paper to learn about area and perimeter
- Graphing and charting based on real objects
- Counting, sorting, and matching using fun objects, items in nature, or ones that are already in their natural environment
- Counting using clothespin clip cards

- Real-life science observation
- Nature journaling
- STEM projects
- Science lab kits such as dissecting owl pellets, starting an ant farm, or raising tadpoles or caterpillars
- Stick-on human body parts or bone labeling
- Kitchen experiments
- Use store-bought interactive models of the human body, a cell, a volcano, or anything else you can think of
- Build your own diagram or model based on any topic. Some ideas include the levels of under the sea, underground animals, planets, layers of the Earth, or an atom.
- Use wooden letters or draw in a box of sand to practice spelling
- Use puffy paint to practice spelling or writing letters
- Use play-doh, pom poms, beads, buttons, or any other objects to trace letters for

letter work instead of only using a pencil, especially for children who aren't ready to use one

- Let your child use a storyboard to reenact a story to show comprehension. This can include the use of a felt board or laminated cardstock glued to popsicle sticks.

My Favorite Homeschool Curriculum for ADHD Learners:

- Evan-Moor
- Funschooling Journals by Thinking Tree Books
- Shiller Learning
- Study.com
- Moving Beyond the Page
- Teaching Textbooks
- Learn Math Fast
- Math-U-See
- Miquon Math
- MasterBooks

- Reflex Math
- JacKris Publishing's grammar, writing, and spelling/vocabulary
- Institute for Excellence in Writing
- Story of the World
- Short Lessons in World History
- All American History
- Bookshark Science
- Generation Genius

Life Skills

At the end of the day, academic skills are often the least of a parent's worry when they have a child with ADHD. Usually, when outsiders think of this type of learning difference, they think of a child who is too hyper or unfocused. Many would assume that attending school would be the greatest hurdle. However, every skill in life has to be taught, not only math, etc.

Parents may be surprised to find out all of the ways ADHD can affect a child's daily life and also how it can impact his/her future as teens and adults. I remember reading somewhere how a child's ability to converse with their peers can also be affected, which gave me answers as to why my child failed to make connections with other kids his age. That is one of those things that doctors, teachers, and therapists did not mention to me when discussing what kind of help my child would need. After reading whatever material I could get my hands on and also connecting the dots in my son's life, I have found that the two major categories of life skills that children with ADHD need extra guidance with are executive functioning and socialization.

Executive Functioning: Skills related to executive functioning are organization, task initiation, self-control/impulsivity, perseverance, attention, planning, and flexibility. I'm sure that you are already aware of many of these if your child has ADHD, but you may not be aware of some. When my son would get upset over the tiniest changes such as me wanting to put the TV remote in a different spot than his "designated area," I had no clue that flexibility was an issue brought on by ADHD. When he would cry and purposely break a project he had just spent hours working on because something didn't go right, I didn't understand why he wouldn't just calm down and let me help him figure it out instead of barging through me to throw it away. Or how his lack of self-control could also lead to destructive behavior when boredom set in, and I would find a torn up chair cushion in his room.

Socialization: My son's lack of socialization skills has interfered with his life since he was a little boy. I remember when I first pulled him out of public school to homeschool, and I saw how much of an issue it was first hand. I already knew that he had a hard time making and keeping friends at school, but I just thought it was the result of his quirkiness and other children being mean to him because of it. The first day I put my son in a homeschool cooperative, I saw another child around his age walk up to him and start a conversation. Expecting my son to converse with this other kid in return, I was stunned when I saw him not say a word and instead, he just simply turned around and walked away as if he was either bored of the conversation or he wasn't paying attention enough to notice them. Lacking self-control to prevent themselves from interrupting when others are talking, appearing to not pay attention to others, randomly switching the topic in the middle of the conversation or saying inappropriate things at the wrong time are socialization side-effects of ADHD.

Over the years I thought long and hard about how to address these issues so that my son could manage life more effectively. I have found that approaching it from a teaching perspective has helped. The skills that are hindered need to be worked on one at a time and need to be treated like a goal to work towards. With goals come objectives. Objectives are the steps it takes to accomplish a goal. Children with learning differences literally need every little step to be broken down and mastered before moving on to the next one. The goal should be tracked and positively reinforced. But how does a parent actually teach these steps? By modeling the preferred behaviors, you wish to see, talking about what's appropriate and what's not and explaining why, and role-playing. With a quick online search, many workbooks available for purchase can be found and offer to teach skills in a variety of topics related to ADHD, such as conversation skills, making friends, and executive functioning. They give scenarios and examples that parents can talk about with their children along with exercises to complete in a short amount of time each day. I highly recommend that parents take advantage of the affordable resources that are available to help their children.

"If we run every class the way we run it for kids with ADHD, we'd probably have a much stronger education system." –Robert Reid

From the earliest days of school life, some children did not "obey" their teachers because sitting still, paying attention, or being quiet were not their strong areas. As time has gone on, educators have become aware of the learning differences that many children have, yet the classroom still has not evolved enough to meet the needs that so many children desperately yearn for…to be fully understood and a system that follows through with that understanding. Following through means changing up expectations, switching to different learning materials, placing an importance on interests, showing children how to use their abilities, and immersing them in nature. Think of how these children would be viewed if changes were made. Would they still be considered as having behavioral problems or attention issues?

Consider these factors when constructing your child's education.

1. What curriculum would you like to further research?

2. What accommodations and interventions would you like to implement?

3. What life skills could your child benefit from practicing?

4. What else might you want or need to learn about ADHD?

Part 9

"Childhood is a short season." - Helen Hayes

Although childhood is short, homeschooling allows more time to enjoy it. It is not just another type of education, but a whole different way of human existence. We have the opportunity as parents and teachers to our children to curate a life for them that most wouldn't be brave enough to try. We are told from the time our children are very young what is "good" for them. As they turn into toddlers, the world is already pushing parents to send their children away. People talk about the importance of structure, independence, and socialization like there is only one way of instilling those things. Many believe that strangers can provide a better learning environment than any parent ever could. When the masses believe something to be true, generations to come will too. The very mention of the word homeschooling causes a numerous number of individuals to shake their heads. If they do not have the opportunity to witness the life changing effects that homeschooling has on children, they may never understand why so many parents are choosing to do so. For the ones who do, they have the delightful privilege of knowing that the everyday lives of children could be so much different. This is true for all children, but especially for ones who do not fit into the mold that the public education system has created.

Traditional schooling with learning differences is not the same as homeschooling with learning differences. When children are allowed to grow in a particular environment that is most nourishing to their needs, they will no longer fail to thrive. A child's day does not have to be stressful from the time he/she wakes up and until the time he/she finishes homework in the evenings. It does not have to force a child to adapt to unrealistic expectations. It does not have to force an unreasonable amount of structure. Most of all, it does not have to significantly hurt their mental well-being.

Rise & Shine

Researchers are aware of how important the correct amount of sleep is for children, yet the environment surrounding them rarely supports this fact. *The American Academy of Pediatrics* reports that only forty-eight percent of children who attend traditional school receive nine hours of sleep, but not on every school night. A doctor involved in this particular study stated that there needs to be a focus on school start and end times.

Children's sleep patterns are directly correlated to academic performance, ability to focus, mental health, and physical health (Au et al., 2014). As children grow older and become pre-teens and teenagers, the amount of sleep needed is even greater, which becomes increasingly obvious when children start to become harder to wake up in the morning. As homeschoolers, children have an advantage over their peers as long as parents don't try to replicate a regular school's schedule too closely. Making yourself aware of the correct hours of sleep your child needs will greatly benefit your child's school day and their life in general. Laura Grace Welding said, "Let them sleep in. Let them dream. Let them wake up to their own possibilities" (Welding, 2012).

Morning Routines

The first part of a child's day can make or break the tone for the remainder of it. No parent particularly enjoys the struggle of making sure all of their children are up, dressed, fed, and ready to start the day, especially when it becomes a stressful time of telling your kids over and over again what they are expected to do. It was mentioned in chapter nine, which focused on ADHD, that instilling self-motivation can more effectively get your child to be more independent. The key is to provide the motivator, which is an hour of uninterrupted free time before any type of educational lesson begins. We as adults love moments to ourselves in the morning, the little bit of time when silence surrounds us, and we are not bothered by anyone else. Our children need that kind of time too. Not only will it serve as a motivator to accomplish their morning tasks, but it will give them time to slow down, relax, and be in a better mood to start school work.

The Lessons

Many parents feel the need to dive right into school work so they can knock out the lessons. I find that children are more likely to *want* to start the school day if a simple activity is prepared that doesn't require as much effort on their end. For example, I might read a chapter book aloud while they doodle, put on an audiobook or video while they put together a puzzle or build something. The reason behind these kinds of activities is that they prepare children to listen while also getting them moving a little bit, which will make the remainder of the school day easier to get into—with less complaints and hopefully raise their attention skills.

Parents can decide how long the simple activity should last. For my children, I plan on taking about a half hour. Once the simple activity is done, then I recommend choosing a lesson that is least preferred by your child since their concentration skills will probably be at their best during this time. Afterward, keep moving from least preferred lessons to most preferred ones. Children will feel that the activities are getting either easier or more interesting to them, which will be more likely to instill a positive attitude and keep them motivated.

Passion Baskets

The full details on passion baskets were mentioned earlier. Refer back to part 6 if needed. William Butler Yeats said, "Education is not the filling of a pail, but the lighting of a fire" (Staff, 2017). Since the beginning, my biggest drive to keep homeschooling my children was not so that I could provide a strict and rigorous education, but to allow the time for them to study a plethora of interesting information and gain skills that would benefit their lives in a way that a "normal" education could not offer. The idea of the passion baskets didn't just fulfill this goal, but other ones too. For example, my kids are motivated to complete their school work so that they can run off and get started on what they love the most. Another unplanned bonus is that I know they are using time more wisely, as opposed to depending on video games or television to give them something to do after daily lessons are done. I'd suggest setting a minimum time requirement such as one to two hours.

Homeschool Groups & Cooperatives

As the number of families choosing to homeschool increases, the topic of socialization still continues to remain the center of concern for those who are not totally familiar with homeschooling. Some parents choose not to homeschool at all because of the socialization factor alone, especially when relatives or friends share their opinions on the matter and try to convince them that school is the only way for a child to be well-rounded and socially accepted. The truth is, homeschool parents are forced to find ways for their children to socialize which often leads them to being more proactive than others in this area of their children's lives. Consequently, homeschool children usually have many things to do and lots of faces to see.

Homeschool cooperatives come in many shapes and forms. Some are free and some require parents to pay an annual or semi-annual membership fee. Cooperatives can also be religious or secular, parent-led or child-led. Many offer academic and extracurricular classes such as algebra or music lessons, while others focus solely on fun activities and just giving the children time to socialize and make friends. Homeschool groups are usually less formal and might stick to field trips, meet-ups, and other activities in various locations. Some may even focus on a specific area of interest, such as nature or arts and crafts. To find homeschool groups or cooperatives, an online search for your area should bring up some results.

What happens when you cannot find a group or cooperative in your area that meets your child's needs or one that is active enough? Many parents find themselves creating their own resources when this happens. In fact, that's why most are started in the first place, because of a parent who is not satisfied with what is already available. Although homeschooling has become more and more popular, resources can still potentially be lacking in certain areas if no parents have taken initiative yet. Some parents may feel that they are not experienced enough to start a group or cooperative of their own, especially if they are brand new to homeschooling. If this is the case, starting a non-formal homeschool group could be a good place to start. All it requires is starting a social media page, thinking of free locations to meet, such as parks or your local library, and coming up with free or very cheap activities for the children to do. Next, you'll want to ask for help from any willing parents to either donate supplies or volunteer their time to help out during group meetings. An additional idea is to set up events that require less from yourself, such as simple park meet-ups or field trips where others just have to pay for themselves.

    I started a free homeschool cooperative a couple of years ago for the middle and high schoolers in my area. My two oldest children don't mix well with other cooperatives or groups because of the large number of young children involved in them and the lack of focus on teen activities. I've arranged a private room at our public library, which many will let people use for free as long as your group does not have any monetary benefit. Since my main focus for the group is to encourage socialization, I set up activities that promote this focus. Games, group projects, team-oriented activities, or anything that allows children to sit and hang out while working on something are what's most important. If you're thinking about starting a group or cooperative of your own, brainstorm what your goals are in doing so. Don't try to mimic other groups or set up activities that your children aren't interested in just to gain more members. Burnout can occur even from running a small homeschool group, so spend your time wisely and don't try to overdo it.

Children don't need a schedule that is constantly busy. Homeschooling allows time for a simpler kind of life. In all aspects of your child's day, always put the quality over the quantity whether it's pertaining to academics, extracurricular, or socialization.

Daily Homeschool Goals

Read Something

Make Something

Learn Something

Enjoy Each other's Company

Laugh Often

Help Someone

Always Try to Improve

Appreciate Where You Are Now

Make Time for Passions

Write your own set of daily homeschool goals below:

Part 10

From Surviving to Thriving

Children shouldn't have to cope at school, they should flourish there.

The decision to homeschool is not taken lightly. That's why many parents might try homeschooling for a while then re-enroll them in school, only to pull them back out again. Parents may know deep down what is best for their child, but the world will try to convince them otherwise, even at the expense of the child's well-being. Children who possess learning differences usually struggle internally for many years whether it's before, during, or after being diagnosed. The diagnosis does not change the environment in which the child is placed in. When you realize your child is not thriving in his/her environment, whether it's a traditional school setting or your current homeschool situation, it can be difficult to move away from what you thought was supposed to be a certain way. You may feel sad that your child is not following your original plan for him/her. Just because something is different though doesn't mean it's worth less than the alternative. Sometimes different is better.

A mother from Washington confided in me about what school was like for her daughter who has specific learning disabilities. She shared some heartbreaking insights about the technique's teachers used on her child to get her to accomplish what was expected from her, despite her being diagnosed with ADHD early on. Behavioral interventions such as having her name clipped down on a behavioral chart, recess privileges taken away, or being forced to turn away and complete school work while the rest of the class was able to watch a movie in front of her are a few examples. The child's mental health had already been impacted greatly at a young age. Her mother recalls her daughter hiding under the kitchen table and making statements about wanting to kill herself because she felt so stupid. As she grew older, she was finally diagnosed with dyslexia, dysgraphia, and dyscalculia. Having some answers was a relief for her mother, but would still not be enough to have her daughter's needs met.

In middle school, a teacher told her, "You don't need accommodations, you just need to try harder." The lack of support from educators led this mother to take matters into her own hands. She learned how to incorporate the proper interventions meant for her daughter's learning differences, such as using the Orton-Gillingham approach for dyslexia. By homeschooling, a new- found confidence was restored that had been lacking for years. As a result, the child has gained a love for learning and an understanding of her own needs and strengths. Today, she wishes to remain homeschooled through high school (M.R, personal communication, February 7, 2023).

Socialization

Someone once told me that homeschoolers are sheltered because parents are able to handpick the social opportunities their children participate in unlike parents who have no control over what goes on at their children's schools. Opposers state that homeschoolers are likely to have more positive experiences, which will not prepare them for the "real world." Society has become so used to the fact that children experience stress, shame, self-esteem issues, and trauma due to bullying or unfair treatment, that they think that's what children need in order to grow into successful adults.

Homeschoolers are social beings like any other person. They crave friends, acceptance from peers, activities that take place outside of their home, and so on. What they do not crave are negative social experiences. If you ask a non-homeschooler which of the two they prefer, it's obvious that these children feel the same way. Bad things will happen no matter where a child goes. That is inevitable. Homeschoolers are not going to be able to dodge every negative bullet that comes their way—that is not the goal. A difference between homeschool parents and non-homeschooler parents is that they are significantly cutting down on the unnecessary poor treatment of their children, because they can! And honestly, who would not want to do that?

Children all have different personality types. Some are extroverted and some are introverted. I've noticed that when a child happens to be both introverted and homeschooled, that child is deemed as antisocial or socially awkward. People also like to blame the characteristics that come with introversion on being homeschooled. Homeschooling cannot change a child's personality type. We are all one or the other for reasons we may never know. Also, there is nothing wrong with being an introvert, as the world needs all kinds of people. Children who prefer to spend a lot of time alone, either working on projects or enjoying their own company, will not be sad and lonely when they grow up. They are the ones who will know how to be happy with just themselves when no one else is around…which is a skill that some never gain.

Final Thoughts

If you're witnessing your child struggle constantly and watching their happiness drain away because of school, it's clear that their education is not only not working, but it's not living up to the potential of your child. Learning differences shouldn't stop a child from attaining a meaningful education or from gaining a love for learning. The special skills that these children hold should be honed in, for they will be what forges a path for them in this world. Build your child up by showing them how to work with their differences and become aware of their interests and strengths, so it will be harder for anyone else, or even themselves to tear them down. The foundation of an education can be the difference between whether a child must cope or are able to flourish.

If your child ever doubts themselves, remind them that they are not meant to be exactly like the others.

They are wildflowers.

YOU BELONG AMONG THE

Wildflowers

YOU BELONG
SOMEWHERE YOU FEEL

Free

-TOM PETTY

Takeaway

1. What aspects of a traditional school are you worried about your child missing out on?

2. How could you help make up for these particular losses?

1. What can your child gain from homeschooling as opposed to traditional schooling?

2. How can homeschooling build a positive foundation for your child's education?

References

A history of the Individuals With Disabilities Education Act. (2020, November 24). Individuals with Disabilities Education Act. https://sites.ed.gov/idea/IDEA-History

Au, Carskadon, Millman, Wolfson, Braverman, Adelman, Breuner, Levine, Marcell, Murray, O'Brien, Devore, Allison, Ancona, Barnett, Gunther, Holmes, Lamont, Minier, ... Young. (2014). School start times for adolescents. Pediatrics, 134(3), 642–649. https://doi.org/10.1542/peds.2014-1697

Cassidy, Sen. B., & Cassidy, L. (2018, December 19). Addressing Dyslexia is key to reducing criminal recidivism. The Hill.https://thehill.com/blogs/congress-b log/judicial/422011-addressing-dyslexia-is-key-to-reduci ng-criminal-recidivism/

Dahl, D. (2022, December 28). 80 ADHD quotes about the neurodivergent way of paying attention. Everyday Power. https://everydaypower.com/adhd-quotes/

Duvall, S. (2022, April 12). Homeschool surge still going strong. HSLDA. https://hslda.org/post/homeschool-surge-still-going-strong

Epstein, V. (2021, November 2). Grade Retention: Is it Good to Hold Kids Back? Kars4Kids Smarter Parenting. https://parenting.kars4kids.org/grade-retention-is-it-good -to-hold-kids-back/

Helen Hayes quotes. (n.d.). BrainyQuote. Retrieved February 1, 2023, from https://www.brainyquote.com/quotes/helen_hayes_1001 59

Hendricks-Weissbach, L. (2023, January 29). The Wait-And-Fail Approach (S. Dersa, Interviewer) [Personal communication].

Horowitz, S. H., Rawe, J., & Whittaker, M. C. (2017). The State of Learning Disabilities: Understanding the 1 in 5. New York: National Center for Learning Disabilities.

Infinity Addiction Solutions. (2022, December 23). The importance of playtime: Why school climbing frames matter. The Good Men Project. https://goodmenproject com/everyday-life-2/the-importance-of-playtime-why-sc hool-climbing-frames-matter/

Jacobson, R. (2016, March 7). How to spot dyscalculia. Child Mind Institute. https://childmind.org/article/how-to-spot-dyscalculia/

Juma, N. (2022, July 13). 80 Les Brown quotes on life, dreams & greatness (2021). Everyday Power. https://ev erydaypower.com/les-brown-quotes-motivation/

Low, K. (2008, April 12). Which learning style fits your ADHD child? Verywell Mind. https://www.verywellmind.com/learning-styles-and-adhd -20551

Macias, L. (Director). (2013). Embracing Dyslexia [Prime Video]. Jason Media.

Math-U-See. (2020, July 6). Math-U-See. https://mathusee.com/

Meldrum, A. (2022, September 21). What is dyscalculia? 7 helpful steps to grasp dyscalculia. Made for Math. https://madeformath.com/what-is-dyscalculia?

gclid=CjwKCAiAxP2eBhBiEiwA5puhNRWWnl2jzmK kMg4QuiDeJ3D1nLCCv8oPgRU_FElmRvCi2-g1UlOj GBoCbisQAvD_BwE

M, R. (2023, February 7). The Road to Homeschooling (S. Dersa, Interviewer) [Personal communication].

Okafor, J. (2021, November 3). 40 wildflower quotes to reflect on moments of beauty. TRVST. https://www.trvst.world/biodiversity/wildflower-quotes/

Oxford languages and google - English. (2020, May 20). Oxford Languages. https://languages.oup.com/google-dictionary-en/

Staff, T. (2017, November 17). 50 of the best quotes about teaching. TeachThought. https://www.teachthought.com/pedagogy/great-best-quotes-about-teaching/

Stuart, J., & Woodard, D. (Directors). (2016, February 9). Class Dismissed [Dvd]. Jeremy Stuart.

The Secret Teacher. (2018, April 7). Secret Teacher: My school dumbs down learning for students with special needs. The Guardian. https://www.theguardian.com/teacher-network/2018/apr/07/secret-teacher-my-school-dumbs-down-learning-for-students-with-special-needs

Thorson, A. (2020, February). February 2020 – dyslexia untied. Dyslexia Untied. https://dyslexiauntied961254870wordpress.com/2020/02

Truman Library Institute . (2014, June 2). Truman quotes. Truman Library Institute. https://www.trumanlibraryinstitute.org/truman/truman-quotes/page/2/

Weldon, L. (2012). Free range learning: How homeschooling changes everything. SCB Distributors.

Wiley. W. When a flower doesn't bloom. (2016, September 1). ACC Docket. https://docket.acc.com/when-flower-doesnt-bloom

Sherrell, Z. (2021, July 21). 6 strengths and benefits of ADHD. Medical News Today. https://www.medicalnewstoday.com/articles/adhd-benefits

Acknowledgments

To my husband, Brian: your love and support are my hidden strengths. You have proven to me that it's true how when the right person is by your side, you can accomplish anything.

To my children: your lives are the inspiration behind everything I do. When I think of my life's success, the first thing that comes to my mind is you. Missy, you are a sweet soul that is wise beyond her years. Spencer, you love everyone unconditionally and are not afraid to show it. Chevy, your curiousness about the world around you makes me excited to be your mother.

To my parents and my brother: thank you for sticking by my side, always jumping to help me without hesitation, and supporting everything I do.

To Grandma Bouverette, Aunt Debbie, Ken, and Bev: even though you are gone now, I can still feel the presence of your love and encouragement.

About the Author:

Shelby Dersa, a resident of Port Huron, Michigan, graduated with a Bachelor of Science in Health and Human Services from Baker College. She had a career providing services to children and adults with mental illnesses and developmental disabilities before working from home full-time as a wife, a mother/teacher to her children, and as a writer. Shelby is the director of the *Blue Water Homeschool Teens Cooperative* and she founded *A Homemade Education* Press. In her spare time, she enjoys cooking, gardening, reading, and going on day trips around Michigan with her husband and children.